"A String Of Beads"

Poems and Memoirs

Of

Shirley Newman

Order this book online at www.trafford.com
or email orders@trafford.com

Most Trafford titles are also available at major online book retailers.

Printed in Victoria, BC, Canada.

ISBN: 978-1-4269-1967-1 (sc)

Library of Congress Control Number: 2009912488

*Our mission is to efficiently provide the world's finest, most comprehensive book publishing
service, enabling every author to experience success. To find out how to publish your book,
your way, and have it available worldwide, visit us online at www.trafford.com*

Trafford rev. 4/1/2010

Trafford PUBLISHING®   www.trafford.com

North America & international
toll-free: 1 888 232 4444 (USA & Canada)
phone: 250 383 6864 ♦ fax: 812 355 4082

Introduction

Straight out, I tell you, I am a poet who also writes short – short stories. Having said that, I want to say too, that if I were to write a book of only poems, people may not read it. Those who seem to be in the know as to what sells say, "POETRY???" If my book were published it would "Maybe" be in the Poetry Section of the bookstore. Note! I said "Maybe". From time to time when I browse in Barnes and Noble, I don't believe I ever saw anyone lift a book from the shelves of the Poetry Section, except me.

It has been my intention since I first began to write seriously, to write memoirs and short stories interspersed with poems. It is not my intention to put one over on my readers, by starting with a story and suddenly have them come upon several poems. I love telling a story and I love writing poems. I love to write them both and I truly hope my readers will enjoy what I have written.

I believe I write for a mature audience, people who have lived for the better part of a century as I have, and can identify with my experiences. At the same time I feel that people in their late thirties, early forties, the ages of my own children, will enjoy reading about my life, various experiences and inner feelings which I find easier to express in writing. My writing may give them better understanding of me and my times.

In fact, that is how it all began. I would tell my daughter something out of my childhood or something about my early years in textile design, or my second career teaching special education in elementary schools. She would be intrigued and she'd say, "Write it down Mom, I'll never remember". So, I began to write and haven't stopped since.

Between my adult children's ages and mine, there are many who might buy my book, if not for themselves, then as gifts for Mother's Day or Aunt Maud's birthday. Maybe one of my stories will appeal to someone who has lived a similar experience or they may give it as a gift to another person who has.

Stories aside, poetry lovers will buy my book just because they like my poems. I think women will buy my book rather than men, though once in the home, I see no reason why men wouldn't pick it up and read it. Witness the men in my writing class who enjoy my poems and stories and admit to it, openly. There are gentle souls among men, those who have a softer side to them. It also depends on who they are buying a book for. The gift should suit the one for whom it is intended. There is a wide market out there, people of varied ages, backgrounds and interests, who will find my book appealing.

My stories and poems are all true, honest, understandable, clear and unembellished. They are me.

Shirley Newman
March 3, 2001

Acknowledgements
In Gratitude

I would like to thank Judy Cullins, who taught my Creative Writing class in La Mesa, California. She encouraged me from the very first day I joined her group in 1997. That day I read several poems after which she said, "We have a poet in our midst." I also want to thank those in the class who offered constructive criticism in the form of feedback each time I read one of my poems or stories. I want to thank Judy Cassis, the teacher in my Creative writing class in Santa Clarita, California, and my classmates in her class. I must give thanks to those who were so kind and helpful, especially Carol Umbehocker, from as far away as Federal Way, Washington. I am extremely grateful to her for all her help and involvement. Also, a thank you to Gerald Brooks. A special thank you to Anita Cohen, who interpreted the computer-ese into English so that I can understand it.

Last, but not least, I have to thank Irene and David Newman whose generous support made this dream of mine become a reality.

Thank you, I love you all, thank you.

Sincerely,
Shirley

A String Of Beads

"Did my grandmother write this book?" Perhaps one day my grandchildren when grown will ask this question. Although written for them, I believe it will have universal appeal, because what is honest and true comes through to the reader.

Here we have "This Is Your Life" type stories which people will relate to, short stories strung together like a bead necklace. The little gold beads in between the larger ones are poems I have written over the years.

Some of my writings will be sad, some will be humorous but all will be slices of life and parts of the heart that will touch everyone.

Shirley Newman
November 1998

Contents

Love Affair

Alexander and Julie met for the first time, last week, in my house, and fell in love.

He invited her to go for a walk.

Hearing laughter, I looked outside. She sat cross-legged on the grass, and he, on the cement sidewalk, facing her. They were building an ant playground. Using twigs, they created a maze and were placing ants within. Both were collaborating, busily absorbed in this project.

Alex, my five year old grandson, active, curious by nature, easily becomes bored when surrounded by adult conversation.

Julie, my thirty-ish year old niece, an accomplished, professional actress with numerous roles to her credit, not even five feet tall, hair pulled back, held by a rubber band, bubbles. She can pass for a teenager with her appearance and effervescence.

I thought, "How many young adults would have the patience, the time, make the effort to play with a little boy and keep him so engrossed and entertained. She was having fun too."

After she left, Alex whispered in his mother's ear, "I love Julie and I want to marry her when <u>she</u> grows up."

February 1, 1997

1

A Chance Encounter

On the train to Los Angeles recently, a woman sat down beside me. We became engaged in conversation, which covered many subjects. I mentioned that on the previous train ride back from L.A., I had written two poems.

"Are you a writer?" she asked. "Let me just say I am a writer in progress", I said.

She told me that she enjoys writing and we talked about that for a while. I mentioned that many years ago I had written a book for my son. "He is adopted," I told her. "When he was small, someone had given me a book. I kept it on the mantel over the fireplace. Frequently, my little boy would point to the book and ask me to read it to him." 'Read me the old book', he would say. "Was the book called <u>The Chosen Baby</u>?" she asked. "Why, yes!" I replied, surprised that she knew the very book I referred to. "I was adopted", she said, "and my mother used to read that book to me." "My son loved that book so much that I decided to write his personal story, patterned after the original. I called it <u>Our Chosen Son</u>."

"Pardon me" a voice said, as a woman came around from the seat behind us. "I couldn't help overhearing your conversation." She squatted, facing us. "I gave up my daughter for adoption by my great uncle. I was fifteen years old at the time." "Since the person who adopted her is a member of your family, do you ever get to see her?" I asked. "Yes, I see her about every three years." "Do you intend to have her back one day to live with you?" "Oh no", she answered, "I couldn't do that to her. He is her father."

At the time, I assumed she meant the girl's adoptive father. Now as I write it, I wonder if maybe this man is her biological father as well. After a short exchange, the woman rose to return to her seat. We wished her well.

My seat partner and I continued our conversation. She told me that she had loving parents and a good life, but out of curiosity and the need to know her health background, she felt she had to locate her biological mother. I told her that I understood because this subject concerns my own adopted daughter as well. When doctors ask her questions regarding family health history, she is unable to answer because she doesn't know.

"For a long time, I hesitated to make inquiries", the woman said, "for fear of hurting my parents. But, then the need to know overcame these concerns. Via the internet, I learned I have two sisters and my mother had died." "Did you ever meet your sisters?" "Yes, I did. We keep in touch and I see them from time to time. I am happy to have sisters, because I was raised as an only child. It is interesting to me to see things we have in common and they tell me I look exactly like my mother."

I don't usually open up to people I don't know, but this day a woman came my way, asked to sit beside me and engaged me in conversation. For the better part of three hours, we talked, listened, empathized, shared and then parted. We never exchanged names, addresses or phone numbers. Our paths may never cross again. It was just a chance encounter, or was it?

October 4, 1998

In Joy Lupoletti's 5ᵗʰ Grade Class, "On Our National Parks"

You each were assigned a poem to write,
About your chosen National Park.
I won't be left out, and become uptight,
So, I'll write one too, just for a lark.

Our parks as you've learned, are yours and mine.
Not one of us owns a bit more than another.
They wait for us to come when we can
To visit and enjoy with father and mother.

Each park is unique, with unusual features,
It's animals, birds and all sorts of creatures.
It's trees and it's plants, it's fantastic flowers,
Can keep us entranced for hours and hours.

The Indian dwellings, the fabulous caves,
The geysers, the lakes will bring on the raves.
Enraptured you'll be with the wealth you'll discover,
Of nature's bounties, you'll become a park lover.

The mountains, the canyons, the falls and the rivers,
The splendor, the majesty will give you the shivers.
So mighty, they are, so grand and so tall.
When you are old, you'll have much to recall.

If we preserve them and follow all rules,
They'll remain as they are, when perhaps we'll return,
With our own sons and daughters. We're not fools
To ruin our treasures. This much we learn.

Be glad you live here in this country of ours.
With all that it offers, the gifts that it showers,
Come see for yourself, enjoy what you see
And let it ever be embedded in your memory.

1977

Misunderstanding

Good friends, old friends
Divided by miles.
Sometimes I wonder,
Have we grown apart?
When was it?
How did it happen?
Have I held onto
The tight friendship
Of years ago,
Refusing to see the signs
That it is not
What it used to be?
I thought we would
Bypass the distance.
What matters is
Heart touching heart,
Caring, sharing as we have.
With all the words
At my disposal, how do I
Find the right ones
That will tell my feelings?

October 18, 1998

5 Haikus

The Symphony

Music fills the Hall.
Billowing, bellowing sounds
I am transported.

The Millpond in Winter

I look at the pond
Frozen over. Red ball day
Children are skating.

The Millpond in Summer

I look at the pond
In summer. Sunday, tiny
Sailboats are racing.

Town Dock

Town dock, late at night
Boats in their mooring, rocking.
A lone man fishes.

Spring

Cold's gone, warmth returns,
Sap flows. Birds sing. Buds burst forth.
Life renews itself.

1975

While Peeling Potatoes

Here is the paper.
I'm holding my pen.
Haven't written a poem
Since heaven knows when.
In a couple of weeks
Classes resume.
What will I read,
When I get to the room?
Must think of something
Or get up and go,
'Cause time is a –wasting.
Well wadda ya know!
Keep it under your bonnet,
Fourteen lines, I've written a sonnet.

August 26, 1999

Old Friends

Bits of paper, yellowed with age
Notes and notations page after page.
Saved over years, for God knows what
As if anyone else cares a lot.

Yet, I must have cared or
I wouldn't have kept them.

Quotes and quotations, poems and rhymes
Those have touched me somehow, at different times.
Some quite silly, others profound,
But like good old friends, nice to know they're around.

January 31, 1997

Cottonwood Falls

Early spring in Laguna Mountains
Runoff from last winter's snow
Waters slide down massive boulders
A sheer curtain of silk tulle veiling
      Fine, almost transparent.

Veering, it falls over and around rocks
Glinting, sparkling crystals
Another turn, and it plays peek-a-boo
Around stones and pebbles
Gurgling, tinkling musical sounds
      Like wind chimes.

All the while from here
Wending its way south
To meet Rio Tijuana in Tecate
Where the waters tango westward
As blended, they dance together to join
      The great Pacific.

August 27, 1999

Inspired by TV program "Afoot and Afield in San Diego"

Five Senses

1. **See** – I look at the flower, admire its beauty.

2. **Smell** – I smell it. Does it have fragrance?

3. **Hear** – It has no sound, only the bees buzzing round it.

4. **Taste** – Some may be eaten, or made into jelly.

5. **Touch** – I pick the blossom and press it. Later, to be worked into a pressed flower picture, where it will be treasured forever.

What A Day It Was

Panic! "I can't find my drum." Mama, Daddy, Arthur and I scurried about looking for it. It was nowhere to be found. "We're late, we must leave now," Daddy said, "or we needn't bother to go at all." Out we went. Daddy closed the door of the grocery store behind us. I was in tears. What would I do without my drum? Only on rare occasions did my parents close the store to go somewhere, but this was my graduation day.

Sewing was not one of my favorite things to do. I was a tomboy then. I loved action. Sitting and doing tiny stitches was not my idea of fun. In fact it was torture.

The boys in my class went to wood working shop. The girls went to the sewing room. Lucky boys making their little benches, while we girls had to make our own graduation dresses and all by hand.

Graduation day was nearing. My dress was far from finished. "You had better work on it," Mama said, or you'll go in your underwear." Toward the end, my friend Gloria came to my rescue. She sewed well and did the final touches. The dress was ugly.

Mama rode the trolley downtown to Losier's Department Store. All department stores then, had an entire floor devoted to sewing, fabrics, patterns, trimmings, sewing machines and supplies. Women sewed more then. Mama bought wide, white satin ribbon for a sash. She had a rosette with streamers made up to attach to the shoulder and a ribbon for my hair.

13

That dress had to be gussied up somehow, in order to make it presentable.

Now, the dress was ready, but I needed white shoes. I wanted high heels in the worst way. Mama said it was not appropriate for a fourteen-year-old. The day before the big day, Daddy took me downtown and we came home with a pair of faille, high-heeled pumps, better suited to a bride.

The school orchestra played "Pomp and Circumstance", "Land of Hope and Glory" we sang, as we graduates filed into the auditorium and took our seats in the front rows. After the usual speeches, each of the graduating classes gave a presentation. My class had prepared a drill, we had rehearsed it for months, the drums six inches in diameter hung in front of us, suspended by a string around our necks. As we marched in precisional cadence, we beat on the drums. We had it down pat.

The time came for my class to be called forward, we went up onto the stage. Everyone lined up with his or her drums in place except me. I was there alright, but no drum. As we went through the steps, I held my hands in position and brazenly pretended to beat on a drum that wasn't there. As we marched, my ankles kept turning and I hobbled through, unused to walking on spike heels.

When it was over, we returned to our seats. A bouquet of flowers was being passed from right to left along my row. I passed it along. Soon it came back from left to right and I passed it on. Then it came back again. I looked at the card attached. Surprise! It was mine. I never had flowers given to me before. "How and when did my parents arrange this?" I cried in disbelief.

After the graduation exercises were over, my parents took me to a photographer where I sat for a portrait. I look at this picture today and laugh. There I sit with the flowers on my lap. The upper part of me with long corkscrew curls, looks like the young girl that I was. The white stockinged legs with those high-heeled shoes look ridiculous. Mama was right. They were inappropriate.

The dress, the shoes, the drum, the flowers, the portrait and all the tears evoke memories of my first graduation. I have never, nor will I ever forget, that day.

February 12, 1997

Joshua

Hi there, sweet angel with your cherub face.
Brightening my world since you came to this place.
What if God had sent you somewhere other?
Like Asia or Africa, not here to join your brother?

What joy I feel when I answer the phone
And hear your laughter as Mommy tickles you.
What pleasure I get when I talk to you, and you respond.
Not yet five months old, and we've begun to bond.

God sent you to us at just the right time
To be named for your grandpa who had just passed away.
I think of his smile if he could see you today.
To kiss you and hold you, in his big blue chair
And run his hand over your silky smooth hair.

I watch you asleep and think to myself
What is in store for this little elf?
How perfect you are and handsome you'll be.
Whatever you become, will be fine with me.

Grandma Shirley
February 2, 1997

To Alexander

My first grandson, "My Beautiful Boy"
Since first you arrived, you've given us joy.
Words can't describe nor feelings reveal
The happiness you've brought, it's hard to conceal.

Mental pictures fill my mind; times you climbed on Papa's lap,
He so tall, you so small, walking together down the street
I coached you to say Grandma, it was Papa, you said first.
That gave him a charge, memories, bittersweet!

You gave him joy in fullest measure.
He'd smile and laugh at things you'd say or do.
He found in you, simply put, pure pleasure.
I know you will remember him, You, yes, you.

Now, you are five and smart as a whip.
Great things are ahead for you, I know and I see.
One of these days, you'll steer a great ship,
Be a man of substance, a credit to our family.
And I'll be so proud, Me, yes, me.

Grandma Shirley
February 5, 1997

In The Throes Of Love

WHO sent you to me? I question,
  Who said, "Let it be done?"
  Who brought us both together?
  The answer can be only one.

WHAT is the magnet that pulls us?
  What is the spell you cast?
  What is this net that enfolds us?
  Dear God, please let it last.

WHEN did you know you loved me?
  When did you see it so clear?
  When did I know it was mutual?
  Why do I want you so near?

WHERE will this love we feel take us?
  Where in the world will it go?
  Where will this road we're on lead us?
  In time we are certain to know.

WHY is this love so exciting?
  Why do I feel like I do?
  Why does my heart beat like thunder?
  The lightning is you, only you.

1999

Conversations With Myself

Come on Old Fool, accept, get a life!
I will, give me time, I've been going through strife.
I just lost my husband; I need time to grieve.
Don't worry, I have many things up my sleeve.

Get up, get dressed, get out and get going.
There are many seeds you need to be sowing.
I know and I shall, all in due time,
But right now I have to find out who I'm.

I've been daughter, student, artist, teacher, wife and mother.
I've always been doing for some "other".
Now, I must learn how to redefine "me".
The journey itself will be interesting to see.

Maybe I'll stumble, maybe I'll fall.
Then pick myself up and grow and stand tall.
Don't push me, don't shove, and with help from above
I'll arrive at the place where I'm destined to be.

February 2, 1997

Ode To John

So young, so handsome
Such promise, so sad

So foolish, so cocky
Unprepared to fly

In such conditions, so dark
Over water, flirting with death

Such chances, how could you?
Your wife, her sister

And you, gone to the sea.
So sad is the nation, the world, and me.

What might you have done,
What might you have been

In the years up ahead,
Had you been more cautious

And used your head?
Too late now to question, to ponder.

Peace for you three
With "Him" up yonder.

July 18, 1999

The Mountains of Miami

Tall, one high-rise after another
Magnificent views of similar buildings
Across the intra-coastal
From the balcony where I sit,
Making these notations, observations.

On the water, boats move,
Some going left, others right.
I become mesmerized.
Boats, all sizes, all kinds,
Each one moving on,
Leaving only their wake.

Years ago, as a guest
At someone's cottage
On a lake in Canada,
I sat on a porch,
Looked at a boulder in that lake.

Sometimes, we went out
In a small boat and fished,
Returning, more often than not,
With empty creel
To sit on the porch,
Look at the boulder in the lake.

Here, today in Miami,
I see people sitting on their balconies
There, across the water,
Watching these boats, their wakes,
And like me, the mountains of Miami.

June 24, 1999

You

Whenever I hear your voice,
It isn't at all by choice.
The senses take over, tis true,
Whenever I think of you.

Whenever I see your face,
No matter the time or place,
I feel our hearts entwine,
Whenever I know you're mine.

Whenever I feel your essence,
The peace, the calm of your presence,
I know I have nothing to fear,
Whenever I know you're near.

The Artist

When you have an artist's nature
  An artist's eye, an artist's soul,
    You apply what you see,
      What you feel, in many ways.

It may be because
  You take the time to see
    And are sensitive to what is around you.

You paint it, arrange it,
  Write about it, photograph it.
    You savor it and save it
      In one way or another.

It could be for your own enjoyment
  Or for others to enjoy
    And appreciate what you saw.

When you dipped your brush in paint
  And lay it on the canvas
    Or put pen to paper and wrote about it
      Or clicked the shutter on the camera,

To capture forever, that scene,
In that light, on that day
At that moment in time.

June 1, 1999

Grandma's Lament

Anita left for home today, taking both my
grandchildren with her.
 Peace
    Quiet
         Everything in place
 Laundry's done and back in the linen closet.
Two sinks full of dishes washed. There are glasses once
more in the cabinet.
Kitchen counters cleared of baby foods, bottles, nipples and
bottle brushes.
 I can see the living room carpet, toys and assorted
children's paraphernalia removed, TV off, no more
Nickelodeon and Disney Cartoons until next visit.
Peanut butter and jelly remnants, wiped up. Nice to have it
  all neat
    and tidy
       but,
 I don't hear Alex saying, "I love you Grandma",
Nor, my daughter's usual "I don't want to go home",
Nor, do I have the little cherub's rosy cheeks to kiss.
Yes, it's
  peaceful,
     still and,
        far too quiet.

March 7, 1997

Bird

If I were a bird and I could fly,
I'd be off and running, into the sky.
Above the world, above the sea,
And I'd say, "Hey, Guys, look at me."

But I'm not a bird.

I'm a people person, for whatever that's worth.
So, maybe there's reason I'm here on earth.
Perhaps, in my next life, if there is such a thing,
I'll come back in a new form, take wing.

And I'll be a bird.

It's a beautiful thought to be soaring and free.
Then again, there are cats who may want me.
So, maybe I'd better stay what I am.
With my feet on the ground, do what I can,

And not be a bird.

March 30, 1997

Remembering Ruth Palmer
and Iroquois Island

What a surprise it was to see Ruth Palmer when I came to the Traphagen School of Fashion on the first day of classes. Ruth and I had attended Erasmus Hall High School in Brooklyn, New York and were graduated the previous June. We knew one another by sight, a nodding acquaintance, you might say, nothing more. Seeing a familiar face in unfamiliar surroundings, in Manhattan, among students from all over the country, we were immediately drawn to one another. Over the next two years, while attending classes in Costume Design, Fashion Illustration, Textile Design and other related subjects, and going out to lunch together, we became good friends in school and outside as well.

The Palmer family owned Iroquois Island, one of the Thousand Islands in the St. Lawrence River, situated between the United States and Canada. When our two years at Traphagen ended, I was invited to go up there for a visit. Ruth drove her aunt's mother and me up to Alexandria Bay. The town, situated on the river, consisted of the usual homes, stores, and the Crossman House Hotel, beside the town dock. Mr. Woods, the caretaker of the Palmer property, met us. We parked the car, transferred luggage to the boat, climbed in and took off. The shortest way to get to the island from town was by boat. Ruth's mother, father, and younger brother had gone up earlier. Her aunt, with her two young children, Norma and Roger and their maid, Nancy, joined us.

As we neared the island, Ruth pointed, "There it is", she said. Talk about culture shock! I couldn't believe my eyes. I saw a big square dock in front with stone pillars in each corner, topped by a lamp, and set way back on the lawn stood the house. To me, a girl from Brooklyn, whose mother operated a grocery store and who lived in a five-room apartment on a trolley-line street, this was an unbelievable sight to be read about in books or seen in the movies. We did not pull up to the front dock but went around to the boathouse where Mr. Woods docked the boat in the middle slip. On the left I saw a yacht, and on the right a smaller boat than the one we arrived in.

I would have to describe the house as a mansion. We entered a center hall and before us a wide staircase led to the second floor. To the left of the main hall were the living room, library and billiard room, each with tremendous stone fireplace, dark wood paneling and high ceiling; to the right, the dining room, kitchen and butler's pantry, with a back staircase leading to the upper floors. Ruth and I shared a huge bedroom upstairs, directly above the center hall. From the bay window, we looked out at the dock and the river.

Mr. and Mrs. Woods, the caretakers had a house of their own behind the big house. They lived there all year round, looked after things, and in summer, when the family came up, prepared the house for their arrival. Mrs. Woods was cook and maid, while Mr. Woods acted as handyman, tour guide, and filled in as needed. Outside, the house had a wrap-around porch. We loved to sit out there and watch the tour boats go by. Every day we heard, "To your right is Iroquois Island, the home of Mr. Aaron L. Palmer of New York City. We waved and the people on board waved back. The opposite side of the island was rocky. We hiked there, then from a boulder dove into the clear, clean water to swim. The Palmers owned the island; no one else lived on it. In back, behind the Woods' little house, there was a small footbridge and a narrow road that led into town, but it was easier and faster to go by boat.

One day, Mr. Woods took us to Gananoque, on the Canadian side of the river. On the way, he pointed out many interesting things. One of the islands was half in the United States and half in Canada. The international boundary line went right through the house. Another island was owned by a man named Boldt. After he married, he had the island dynamited into the shape of a heart. He had a home built, known now as Boldt Castle, but before it was completed, his wife died. He never finished it, never lived in it, and to this day it remains as it was.

I learned how to pilot the boat and how to avoid the shoals. Some days, Ruth's friend François came to the island. We took the boat out into the river and there Ruth and François taught me to aquaplane. Evenings, after dinner, Ruth and I dressed up and took the small boat into town. At the hotel, a live band played every night for dancing. People came in their boats, tied up at he dock and went in for dinner and dancing. Along with hotel guests and people from the vicinity, François and his friends joined us there. When it came time to leave, the boys walked us to our boat. Ruth said, and I have never forgotten her warning, "You never allow a boy to take you home because you can't say 'no' in a boat".

One morning at breakfast, Mrs. Palmer said, "this evening we will have a costume party. The rule is: you cannot go into town to buy anything, be creative; use whatever can be found in or around the house". We all got busy scrounging around, then went to our rooms to prepare for the evening. Everyone was secretive about what they came up with. I am laughing as I write this, picturing again the scene as each of us came down the grand staircase, through the wide doorway and into the living room, bowing and waving to the laughter and hand clapping of an appreciative group.

Ruth wore a sheet draped like a toga, with a wreath of daisies in her hair; a woodland nymph. I found a long white apron, tucked up one corner into the waistband, piled my long red hair into a knot on top of my head, got a bucket and mop and was a washerwoman. Ruth's mother wore one of her son's horizontal striped shirts which was much too tight for her, a beret on the side of her head, and a short black skirt, slit on the side, an apache dancer—and, yes many of her teeth were blacked out. Following the costume parade, we all went into the dining room for dinner.

One day, amid the fun and frolicking, a telegram arrived at the house. It was from my mother telling me my younger brother was in the hospital and I would have to come home. I immediately made arrangements to take the train back to New York City. The next day, another wire arrived saying, "Stay at the island if you want to. Letter will follow." But I knew I was needed at home, so with great reluctance, I left these dear people and this wonderful place.

Ruth and I remained friends for several years. After that memorable summer our paths went in different directions. She met and married a young man named Sid Gusar, a pharmacist who owned his own business in Monticello in upstate New York, where they settled. Ruth never pursued any aspect of the fashion industry.

In the fall of that year, I began to work as a textile designer and followed that career for almost ten years. Meanwhile, Ruth and Sid had two children, and moved to Florida where she wrote that they built her dream house around a swimming pool. We continued to correspond for some time, then fell out of touch. I never saw Ruth again after she moved to Florida, although I thought of her often. A few years ago, on a whim, I decided to write to her. I told her briefly about my life since we last corresponded and I reminded her of some of the fun times we had in the past. I told her how I often thought of her and how I would like to hear from her.

One day I received a phone call from a woman named Sylvia Gusar who told me that a lovely letter came to her house addressed to Ruth Gusar. She felt she had to reply to it. "Ruth died of cancer several years ago," she said. "I was widowed at about the same time. Sid and I were married shortly after we met and two years ago, he passed away. I have remained in the house you mentioned." I inquired about Ruth and Sid's children, now grown and out on their own. I asked about members of Ruth's family. Sylvia impressed me as a lovely woman. I thanked her for calling…so considerate of her. I felt sad and sorry that I waited so long to rekindle my friendship with Ruth.

July 13, 1999

Potato Roesti

Now here's a recipe that looks delish.
You fry it up crisp and set on a dish.
Top with Caviar and Sour Cream.
Mmm! Sounds like a dream.

Can't go out and buy it.
So I might as well try it.
Come on folks, it's ready to eat.
Ooh, this is good! What a treat!

March 30, 1997

God's Promise

Israel, land of my ancient Ancestors
Dispersed, displaced in foreign lands
Ever yearning to reverse the course
Come back to their homeland, over desert sands.

Return many did, over centuries and war.
To reclaim what was theirs, in times of yore
Before Jerusalem was sacked, Holy Temple destroyed,
Western Wall remains, Israel is reborn, spirits ever buoyed.

Those who did not, for whatever their reasons
Still felt in their hearts, their spiritual home.
"Next year in Jerusalem", we pray in all seasons.
May our people in the future, nevermore need to roam.

We dare not, we must not, just give up our land
To those who would have us fall into the sea.
It's our haven, our hope, we must stretch out our hand.
But only with complete assurance of our security.

Though I am not there, I wish safety and peace
For all of my brothers who found ways to arrive.
We know in our hearts, hostilities, must cease.
Find ways to do it. *ISRAEL MUST SURVIVE!*

1997

Peony

In Port Washington, where
I lived for thirty-three years,
I had a row of peony plants.

   When in bloom, they were
   A sight to behold. Each flower head
   An orb, five inches across.

But oh, the color, bright, brilliant pink.
So vivid! No wishy-washy shade
But a true, shocking pink.

   And oh, the scent, fresh, sweet
   But not that cloying sweetness,
   Just a delicate, delicious fragrance.

How I loved to cut some
Of those long stems and
Bring them inside to admire,

   Before the heavy heads
   Bent their stems over
   And made the lovely flowers

Bow down, their season so short.
Year after year they bloomed
And gave me infinite pleasure.

How sad, when I moved away
And left those faithful friends
For the new occupants of my house.

November 16, 1999

Autumn In Maine

Helen and I sit on a swing,
Which hangs from a branch of an old oak tree.
It's peaceful, still, and my heart sings.
I'm mindful of God's gifts to me.

Our friendship shared over many years
And now we're together to reminisce,
Good times, sad times, laughter, tears
Enjoy nature's bounty, nothing's amiss.

We look out at the cove, admire the scene
Hear the lap of the water, coming on shore.
Trees bent over, leaves falling down and in between
Birds fly and sing a melodic score.

Country roads, wide open fields,
Cattails, wild asters, and Bittersweet
Proudly offer abundant yields.
Dried grasses and fallen leaves cushion our feet.

The colors of leaves against the sky,
Reds, yellows, greens and golds
A visual feast for my artist eye
Autumn's generosity truly unfolds.

We take pictures of each other in interesting places.
We walk and talk about memories past.
Meanwhile, creating new ones to fill in the spaces,
All of which, will have to last...

Until we meet again.

January 2000

In My Twenties

We were textile designers, my best friend and I. Not only did we spend the working day together, but after work we did things together too. "Let's go to Macy's and try on hats," and we did. Macy's, on Herald Square in mid-town Manhattan, had a big millinery department with many hats on display. We'd try on the most ridiculous hats and crack up with laughter. We sometimes pooled our pennies and went to Romeo's for a twenty-five cent plate of spaghetti. It was wartime. When we could think of nothing better to do, one of us would say, "Let's go to Penn Station and kiss the boys goodbye," and we did.

After we got home from work, or wherever we'd gone afterward, we'd call one another. My mom used to say, "You two are like the two women who were in prison together for ten years. When finally they were released, one said to the other, "Meet me on the corner tomorrow, I have something to tell you."

We were in our twenties, unattached, carefree and spontaneous. One day, after the office holiday party, Debby said, "How about hopping on a train and going down to Washington?" Her sister lived there. "O.k., let's!" And away we went, with just the clothes we had on. Once there, I called my mom. "Guess where I am…, Washington, D.C." Slam! She banged down the receiver. Another time, on the spur of the moment, we went to Hartford, Connecticut. Jerry, who I married after the war, was stationed there. He got his army buddy for Debby and they met us at the train station in Hartford, Conn." I called home, "Mom, guess where I am…Hartford, Conn." Bang went the receiver. Mom did not like her children to sleep away from home ever, not even at a friend's house.

I have always felt that being twenty-five and single was the best time of my life, old enough to do what I wanted with no one to account to, except my mom of course. I felt I had to let her know where I was so that she wouldn't worry when I didn't come home.Nowadays, I take my time making decisions. But back then, we acted on impulse and those times were some of the best times. When Debby and I get together, we recall and laugh about the crazy things we did, lo, those many years ago.

October 7, 1999

What's In A Word

Page 1.

Words Can:
> Bring laughter
> Cause tears
> Express sympathy

Words Can:
> Cheer
> Compliment
> Teach

Words Can:
> Raise spirits
> Evoke sadness
> Bring joy

Words Can:
> Antagonize
> Chastise
> Anger

Words Can:
> Paint pictures
> Hurt
> Torment

Words Can:
> Preach
> Reach heights
> Touch hearts

Words Can:
> Singe
> Calm
> Insult

Words Can:
> Show understanding
> Win friends
> Lose friends

Words Can:
    Placate
    Debilitate
    Corroborate

Words Can:
    Give hope
    Give meaning
    Describe

Words Can:
    Please
    Tease
    Soothe

Words Can:
    Titillate
    Intoxicate
    Penetrate

Words Can:
    Bring gladness
    Cause pain
    Be mean

Words Can:
    Exhilarate
    Elevate
    Make sense

Words Can:
    Lure
    Cure
    Sing

Words Can:
    Blow minds
    Spellbind
    Be kind

Words Can:
    Traumatize
    Mesmerize
    Eulogize

Words Can:
    Raise doubts
    Ease stress
    Cause stress

Page 3.

Words Can:
    Chill
    Say too much
    Say too little

Words Can:
    Patronize
    Exaggerate
    Aggravate

Words Can:
    Console
    Confuse
    Inform

Words Can:
    Influence
    Gratify
    Forgive

Words Can:
    Tell Truth
    Lie
    Endure

Words Can:
    Falsify
    Satisfy
    Endear

Words Can:
    Belittle
    Tickle
    Defend

Words Can:
    Clarify
    Pacify
    Explain

October 1998

Wordplay

Words can be:

Heartwarming	Antagonizing
Heartrending	Calming
Never ending	Energizing
Sinful	Critical
Harmful	Topical
Hurtful	Angry
Loving	Belittling
Kind	Deceiving
Pathetic	Charming
Sympathetic	Mesmerizing
Warm	Deflating
Plain	Inflating
Simple	Traumatizing
Fanciful	Tormenting
Cheerful	Plentiful
Meaningful	Artful
Understanding	Sparse
Threatening	Chilling
Enduring	Clarifying
Useless	Thoughtful
Senseless	Forgiving
Insulting	Unforgiving
Hopeful	Placating
Truthful	Nullifying

Informative

Luring

Enticing

Spellbinding

Intoxicating

Titillating

Pleasing

Consoling

Gratifying

Qualifying

Asinine

Expressive

Possessive

Repressive

Forthright

Elevating

October 1998

Crossroads

Our paths crossed.
We touched briefly
and moved on.
In some strange way,
each of us left his mark
upon the other.

1950

Last Class

We've come to classes faithfully,
As health and time permitted it.
We've toiled and pondered endlessly,
Wrote, revised, rewritten it.

Made copies for our classmates,
Then read in class our masterpieces.
Graciously received the feedback
And come to the day when this class ceases.

We've earned our rest and relaxation,
Turning attention to other pursuits.
Perhaps, even going on vacation
Or rounding up some new recruits.

But oh, though Thursdays "one to four",
For now are free to do other things,
The wheels in our minds keep on turning,
Pushing our pens, as the garden bird sings.

So, come July when we return,
For summer classes we'll be prepared,
To read again our new endeavors,
Carefully written and joyfully shared.

May 24, 1998

How I Handled Change In My Life

Five months after our fiftieth wedding anniversary, my husband passed away. I needed time to grieve, time to adjust, and time to take care of the many details involved in transferring from our names to mine. All that paper work helped with the grief, because there was so much to do that it left little time for feeling sorry for myself. The times when the loss and sadness washed over me, I took in stride and busied myself with painting and writing.

Several months later, I joined a Creative Writing class and took painting classes as well. Getting out, going to class, mingling with others with similar interests, was uplifting.

I had dabbled in both these creative pursuits off and on, over the years. Now, with my husband gone and my children married and on their own, I had the time and the desire to pursue writing seriously, and painting, when I felt moved to do so.

This is how I handled the greatest change in my life. My advice is : Get involved in something that you enjoy doing. Stick with it. Work at it. Keep your mind active.

Six years have passed since I began to write seriously. I have written over two hundred poems and short stories and hope soon to have them published in a book.

July 16, 2003

Moments of My Life

"Life is not measured by the number of breaths we take, but by the moments that take our breath away." This quote by George Carlin reminded me of another I heard recently in an interview on T.V. I heard Elie Wiesel say, *"Life is not made up of years, it is made up of moments."*

I stopped to think. What were the great moments in my life and which of these great moments took my breath away? I reached for my trusty yellow legal pad and my pen, never too far from my fingertips and began to make a list.

1. My Wedding
2. Our first house
3. Our first car
4. Our trip to London & Israel
5. The trip across the United States
6. Adopting our son Charles
7. Adopting our daughter Anita
8. Anita's Wedding
9. The arrival of our grandsons, Alexander & Joshua
10. Backtracking, my two careers, Textile Designing and Teaching
11. Our two businesses: Bayles Drug Store and Suburban 5 & 10
12. Places I've lived, Brooklyn, N.Y., Port Washington, New York, San Diego, California and Valencia, Ca.

This reads like an outline of my life, and, in a way it is. There were many events along the way and many highlights, but, the one that stands out above them all was the incomparable joy I felt the day I brought my son from Canada to his new life in the USA, to his home in Port Washington, New York with Jerry and Shirley Newman, now and forever, his parents.

How I Got Started

From time to time, I would tell my daughter some anecdote from my past, or quote something that my mother said. Mama had a lot of sayings. As I get older, I find myself using those sayings quite often, e.g.: "The Apple Doesn't Fall Far From The Tree", etc. Each time, my daughter would say, "I'll never remember. Mom, write it down."

One day I began to make notes. When I would recall an incident, I added it to the list. Soon the list grew into pages.

I decided shortly after to join a class in Creative Writing. One day, our teacher asked us to write a time line. "Write down the numbers from one to ten, then, beside the numbers, starting with your birth, write down events in your life. Then go on from ten to twenty, and so on." I got as far as fourteen when she said, "Now pick one of the things on your list, and write something on it for next week." I chose my Elementary School Graduation Day and titled it "What a Day It Was". I read it in class, the following week.

Today, March 14, 1997, I dressed after breakfast, intending to go out to do my errands. Instead, I sat down with a pad in front of me, took pen in hand and started to write. I never did go out. It is now 7:31 P.M. and except for time out for a hot dog on a bun and several cups of tea, I have been writing all day. I am bleary eyed. I'll stop here and perhaps go on with it another day.

P.S. I did get back to that story two years later, and finished it on November 17, 1999. It is the story about my mother, which I called "Dora".

December 18, 2003

In My Forties

The turning point in my life, a major change, came shortly after my 40th birthday.

We had been married twelve years without children, not by choice, when word reached us that soon a baby would be born and available for adoption. With this announcement, the life we had known up to that point changed drastically.

We became consumed with the adoption process. Difficult enough within our own country the United States, ours involved Canada. Undaunted, we forged ahead. It took ten months to overcome the stumbling blocks, legalities and obstacles that were placed in our way before we could bring our son from Canada, to our home in the United States. Five years later we went through an almost repeat performance when we had the opportunity to adopt our daughter. This time being experienced we avoided many of the obstacles, so that this adoption went much smoother.

From a twosome, we became a family with all of the ramifications that "Family" entails. My 40's were the busiest, happiest, most exciting and rewarding time of my life.

October 28, 1999

My Dream

I awoke, looked at the clock – 8:45 A.M. I had been dreaming. I felt my shoulder to see if I still had the Nicoderm Patch there. I pulled it off!

The instructions on the Nicoderm box say, "Wear the tape for sixteen hours and remove it. If you have a strong craving for a cigarette in the morning you can leave the patch on twenty-four hours."

Several times, perhaps four, with the patch left on, I have had frightening dreams. After the last time I had one, I thought "It may be the patch, feeding me nicotine during my sleep. When I smoked, I did not get nicotine during the night. I must remember to remove it before going to bed," but, sometimes I forget.

In all of these dreams, including last nights, I am lost in a strange place and cannot find my way home. None of the places are the same. I try to find help, get directions. When I do find someone and I try to ask, I have no voice. If I try to scream, nothing comes out. If I do make some sounds it is garbled.

Later, when I am awake, I reason that I may be trying to scream and the sounds are unclear, just as when you hear someone talking in his sleep and cannot make out what he is saying. A sort of babbling. But, always I am lost, nervous, anxious, frightened and when I try to speak, I have no voice. I wake up shaken. My heart pounding and it takes me a while to calm down.

I think, "I should write this down", but, I get busily involved in my day and it is forgotten. Not completely though – I can't remember the details of the dream, but, I do remember the helplessness and the fright in the dream and how upset I feel when I wake up. At those times, I think, "A person could have a heart attack or a stroke, while sleeping".

In last nights dream, still fresh on my mind, I have left my sister-in-law and my husband in her shop and gone out for something. (Doris has no shop.) Next, I am on the telephone. Doris tells me Aunt Dora is there and wants to talk to me. I tell Aunt Dora to be sure to wait for me, and that I will be back in a few minutes. (Aunt Dora? She has been dead twenty-five years.) I walk up one street, down another and cannot find my way. I realize I am lost. I stop and ask for directions to 103 Zorba Street. (Zorba Street? Where did this come from?) No one seems to know or maybe they do not understand my muttering.

I see small conveyances, something like a three wheel motorcycle, driver in front and one seat in back. I hail one, get in, and tell the driver, "103 Zorba Street". I figure he'll just make the right turn and have me back where I need to be in a jiffy. Instead, we are riding away from the area. I feel very nervous. Finally, he stops in front of a house. I realize I don't have my purse with me. All I have is a one dollar bill and some change in my pocket. He will not accept that. And at the same time, I am aware that I should keep it, in case I have to make a phone call. I am frightened.

Now I am inside the house. There are two women there in cotton house dresses. I make my way out, squeeze through the slats of a wooden gate. The women are trying to stop me. I panic and run, trying to find help.

I see a woman at an outside phone. I ask her if she can tell me how to get to 103 Zorba Street. All the while I am aware that my speech is unclear. As she turns toward me, she says,

"Here comes a policeman". I feel relief. He will be able to get me back.

As he approaches, I see he is not in uniform. This worries me, but okay, he could be off duty. He is a pleasant enough looking man, perhaps in his late fifties. I tell him where I want to go. We walk. He stops to greet people along the way. Everyone seems to know him and like him. I feel he is no threat, but, still I am nervous and anxious to get back, and he is in no hurry. He is just ambling along.

It is starting to get dark and my husband will be worried and probably Aunt Dora could wait for me no longer. I try to convey this to him. My speech is garbled. I am frustrated.

He stops at a beauty salon. The woman proprietor greets him warmly. She shows him a crafts item, a doll. They chat. I wait. We go on, but, he keeps stopping to talk to everyone along the way. My heart is beating very fast. I am growing more and more agitated. Why is he dawdling? I feel this great urgency to get back and I don't know how, without his help.

Now we are in the downtown section of this city. There are tall buildings and an old red brick ornate building. I look at the architecture. I don't recognize any of it except for a Chinese department store which Doris once pointed out to me. (not so) We enter. He walks over to a counter and is smiling and chatting with the man and woman behind the counter. He knows them. I am impatient. I look at a baby romper on the counter and think, "This would be nice for the baby, Joshua, my grandson".

Just then, a woman, seated on a stool in front of the counter next to where I was standing, turns toward me. She has on a dark winter coat with a big fur collar and a white cotton floppy brimmed hat. I am startled by the outfit. An elegant coat and a hat that someone might wear working in the garden as protection from the sun. I stare. It is my mother. I see my brother Morton behind her left shoulder. She and I are excited to see one another. We throw our arms around each other's shoulders and necks, grabbing one another, hugging and kissing and crying all the while. (My mother died 27 years ago.)

I woke up. My heart was pounding and I was still shaken. I got out of bed, went directly to the kitchen, sat down and wrote this account. I never did get back to 103 Zorba Street, and I will leave a note on the kitchen counter hereafter, to remind me to remove the patch before I go to bed.

P.S. I re-read the instructions on the Nicoderm box. It says, "If you begin to have vivid dreams while wearing the patch twenty-four hours, try removing it at bedtime.

Monday, May 12, 1997

Dreams

Dreams:
    Crazy
        Mixed up
            Weird

Scenes:
    Pictures
        Places
            Disconnected

People:
    Unknown
        Known
            Filter In

Emotions:
    Strong
        Disturbing
            Distressing

Where do dreams come from?
Why do we dream?

May 6, 1997

Baja

How good to get to Cantamar,
Even though the drive is far.
What a lovely glorious day.
Let's give a cheer and shout "OLE".

Away from the humdrum, away from care,
Dinner at Jacks, no wear and tear.
What a nice way to spend with friends.
Hope this "FIESTA' never ends.

May 29, 1997

Pondering

If I could do it all over again
    What would I change?
        What would I do differently?

And if I changed a lot of things,
    And if I did them differently,
        Would I be a better person?

Would I have led a better life?
    Would I have been happier?
        Would I have contributed more?

How will I ever know?
    When will I be told,
        Or when will I be shown?

If ever I get to heaven,
    (I don't think I've earned the other place)
        Will all my merits be tallied
            When "WE" come face to face?

And is there really a hell or heaven?
    Maybe I'll never find out.
        So, I guess I'll just plod on
            And continue to mull over this doubt.

June 23, 2000

Coney Island

Our grocery store was hot and the kitchen behind it even hotter. It had no window, no air conditioning. The only air coming in was through the front door of the store.

On those dog days, we begged Daddy to make a pot of orange lemonade. He put in a big chunk of ice. We dipped our glasses in, filled them with the cold orangeade and drank. Daddy cut a cardboard square from one of the cartons and used it as a fan.

Daddy couldn't take the heat. I must really be his daughter because I hate the hot weather too. When Mama saw that it got to him, she'd say, "Take the children to Coney Island." It didn't take us long to get ready. Meanwhile, Mama prepared our lunch.

Our store was on a trolley line. We waited out in front for the trolley and rode it downtown to Flatbush Avenue Extension. There we went down to the subway and took it to Stillwell Avenue, the last stop, Coney Island. As we neared Stillwell Avenue it miraculously became an elevated train. That amazed us. We went down the steps to a large area of concession stands with all kinds of souvenirs, beach toys, drinks, and bags of Bonomo's Salt Water Taffy. Daddy bought us tall narrow glasses of buttermilk. I can still remember how we enjoyed that cold drink after the long trip from home to our destination.

From the station we walked along Surf Avenue to Ravenhall Baths or Washington Baths. Daddy paid the admission at the ticket booth and we were given the keys to our locker rooms. We had individual dressing rooms. I went to the Ladies, Arthur and Daddy to the Men's. We changed into our bathing suits, hung our clothes on hooks, shut the doors and met near the pool. The keys hung from an elastic band which we twisted, on our wrists or ankles.

We preferred going to the pool with Daddy rather than Mama. All Mama did was go into the shallow water and dunk up and down. That wasn't much fun. Daddy was a good swimmer. He dove off the high board into deep water, then swam breaststroke over to the side where we were waiting for him. We took turns jumping into the deep water and when we rose to the surface, he was there to catch us and tell us what a good job we did. He gave us confidence and taught us not to be afraid of deep water. One at a time, he taught us to swim. First he held his hand under our bodies, from time to time removing it, until we learned not to rely on his hand being there. He taught us the backstroke, overhand, breaststroke and how to float.

When lunchtime came, we picked up our lunch from the locker and went to a table in the eating area. Daddy always started with a bowl of hot Manhattan clam chowder. Mama had packed salmon sandwiches, whole tomatoes with a little packet of salt, hard-boiled eggs, fruit and cookies. We bought milk or sodas. Daddy ordered coffee. After eating we had to wait to digest our food before we could go back onto the water.

Behind the pool a passageway under the boardwalk led to the beach. We went out there to play in the sand. Together we built some neat sandcastles complete with moats. Sometimes we went into the water but only up to our knees. When Daddy said it was okay, we went back to the pool.

Sometimes we stayed late when there was a water show. There were races and diving contests but what we kids loved best of all were the clowns on the greased pole. We howled with glee as the clowns tried to keep their footing but invariably slid from the poles in the craziest positions and with funny expressions on their faces.

On most days, we left the pool about five p.m., went to the locker room, took cold showers (there was no hot water), got dressed, met outside the locker rooms and went to walk on the boardwalk.

The boardwalk was lined with booths, all kinds of things to eat, souvenirs, games of every kind, rides. Daddy being as big a kid as we were, indulged and allowed us to eat hot dogs and fancy cut French fries which were called potato chips. We put on lots of salt and ketchup. For dessert, we had either ice cream sandwiches on hot waffles or frozen custard, (something like today's soft ice cream) only, as I remember it, it was much better back then.

When we were full, we walked to the merry-go-round taking outside horses so that we could grab for the brass rings as we rode by. We never rode the Cyclone, Coney Island's famous roller coaster, mainly because it was expensive (twenty-five cents) but also because I was afraid of it. We did stop to listen to the screams and watch people coming off, looking pale and "green around the gills," Daddy said.

It was dark as we walked along Surf Avenue passing lines of people at Nathan's Hot Dog Stand waiting for their treats, and farther down and across Surf Avenue we watched the evening revelers entering Luna Park as we headed for the train station and home – Daddy and two very tired but happy children.

I will never forget those days at Coney Island.

One

When two individuals become one,
Don't lose your individuality,
Just because someone says,
"You must love, honor and obey".
Now that you are one, be autonomous.

One? Yes, you are one and he is one.
Both together are one couple.
A couple is a pair, and a pair is two.
Two ones.

Each one is separate, though together,
Ideally with a common goal.
Yet, each person's thoughts are his
 Or her own. Unique! Valid!

March 25, 2000

Trying

April Fools Day, day one on "The Patch":
Ash trays away, lighters as well,
Threw out ten cigarettes. Determined? Natch!
Though sometimes I feel I want to yell.

I go to the drawer where they were kept.
I look in my purse for the other pack.
Force of habit. I need to accept,
They're no longer there. I'm a sad, sad sack.

I told myself I was under stress.
"Not now", I said. One more excuse.
Time went on and I had to address
The simple fact it was substance abuse.

I'm fighting the fight to lick this affliction,
This nicotine addiction. Eating my fill
Of all kinds of candy and anything handy.
If one thing won't kill me, the other one will.

Well here I am, it's now day ten.
I'm trying so hard. Hope to succeed.
Can't say that I won't, ever again.
One day at a time, without that weed.

1997

Still Struggling

Not "pretty easy" to stop smoking,
Not very easy at all.
It's damn hard; I'm not joking.
Fear I may head for a fall.

Made the decision to quit.
Determined to persevere
When having a nicotine fit.
Glad no one is around to hear.

I take the suggested deep breath,
Wait for the candy to melt,
Stave off what could be my death,
One more day under my belt.

It's not just the patch for ten weeks.
That's only the start of the fight.
It's what comes after that counts.
Will I have the strength and the might?

"Stick with it," I say to myself.
Only two more weeks to go.
Will I make it? What do you think?
For I sure as hell don't know.

1997

Pre: Smoking Paranoia

When I was a young woman in my early twenties, smoking was a sophisticated thing to do. All the movie actresses did it. These were my role models.

I lived in New York and worked as a textile designer in New York City. I held my paintbrush in my right hand and a cigarette in my left hand. Smoking was accepted. No one minded, no one complained because everyone did the same. Monsieur Charbonnet, the designer who sat in front of me, the same one who taught me French as we worked, smoked a pipe. No one had to leave the studio to go out for a smoke.

The top of our tabourets, to the right of our drawing tables held a jug of paintbrushes, jars of water, bottles of tempera paints, and always an ashtray.

No one told us not to smoke, no one asked us not to, no one coughed, choked, or complained of being allergic.. No one was paranoid.

In the tall mid-town Manhattan skyscrapers where I worked, people rode up or down in elevators, smoking: no dirty looks, no ugly glances, no snide remarks.

Where did all these allergic people suddenly come from?

A Country Scene

Come along with me
as we step over the frame
and into this painting.

Let us stroll
through the field of golden wheat,
and feel it sway in the gentle breeze.

How cool in the shade
of the ancient oak,
with its branches spread wide.

We can only catch glimpses
of the blue sky above,
through the canopy of leaves.

Off to the right, notice fields of gold and green.
Up ahead, a red house, a barn
and outbuildings cluster beside the road.

In the distance, see the foothills,
a forest of pines raising its arms
to touch the sky.

Let's pause for a moment
inside this peaceful country setting,
to savor the calm that surrounds us.

March 31, 2000

A Kiss, What Is It?

PHYSICALLY:
A pair of lips coming in contact with:
    A forehead, a cheek
    A baby's foot, a boo-boo
    A puppy, a kitten
    The ground....or....ah!
    Another pair of lips.

EMOTIONALLY:
    A token of love
    An expression of feeling
    A spontaneous act
    That sets your head reeling.
    Awakens your heart
    When it gets zapped
    With visions of passion
    Yet untapped.

October 20, 1997

How I Would Rather Spend My Time.....

"Housework rots the mind." I saw this on a greeting card, bought it and kept it on the fridge for several years. Those words struck a chord. Housework is the most unrewarding thing I can think of. It is ongoing, never ending and a waste of precious, sacred time. No sooner do we finish dusting, and then the nasty film begins to grow again, like a fungus.

My mother said, "When you are a housewife, all you do is take things from one place and put them in another". This is true. You take dishes from the cupboard, set the table, remove the dishes, put them in the dishwasher, empty the dishwasher and put the dishes back into the cupboard.

You take clothes from the closet, put them on, remove them in the washing machine, take them from there, put them in the dryer, take them out, fold or hang them and put them back in the closet.

Now that I'm writing this, I realize that Mama was right on. She summed it up in few words. That is exactly what we do, take from one place and put in another. As I grow older, I find myself quoting her more and more. Why didn't I realize when I was younger, just how smart she was? There used to be an advertisement where the woman with her starched little apron had just finished washing her kitchen floor. She stands there in ecstasy, admiring the shiny floor. REALLY! It's only going to get tracked up again the minute the kids come in.

I do like a neat and clean house, I must admit, but I don't go into a trance when it is done. The truth is I resent it because there are more creative and rewarding things I'd rather be doing with that time. It is just a necessary evil. To my way of thinking, there is nothing elevating about cleaning house.

One of my creative pursuits is making pressed flower pictures. I find something spiritual in flowers, one of God's creations. I love them in the garden, but when I pick them, press them, and make them into a work of art, this is gratifying. It nourishes my soul. How can housework compare?

Once completed, set under glass in a frame, it will be treasured forever. The flowers at their peak, painted not by me, but by God. When given as a gift, the receiver gets a one-of-a-kind piece of art with part of the giver in it, hands, eyes and heart, and a gift from God as well.

March 17, 1997

I Feel Spring Coming

It is one of those clear days
when the sky is blue, so blue
with not a cloud in sight.

Far off in the majestic Rockies
I see the snow, which the warmth
of approaching spring has not yet melted.

The river bubbles along
carrying run off that
trickles down from the mountains.

The banks of the meandering stream
bordered by yellow blossoms
of nature come to life.

Even delicate branches
amid the flowers
show signs of awakening.

From river to mountains, the plains
turn green, that fresh green that we see
at no other time of the year.

Spring…
   Season of hope,
      Birth,
         Renewal.

                        March 31, 2000

Only Through The Eyes Of A Child

A Christmas tree, a Menorah of gold
Branches outstretched, memories unfold
Of holidays past, when we were small
And we gazed at those symbols standing tall.

We held our breath as candles were lit
In awe, awaiting our holiday gift
So anxious we were, we could hardly sit still.
Those times are long gone, against our will.

For children, the wonder and excitement's the same.
For us, that's all changed, it's part of the game.
Only in the presence of a child, can we briefly recapture
That fanciful feeling, that joy and that rapture.

December 3, 1997

Chanukah

From generation to generation, "Dor L'Dor,"
The miracles of Chanukah have been passed along
Even in peacetime, even in war
Told in story, sung in song.

In the bosom of home, safe from harm
Or on the battle fields where soldiers fall
Whether in soothing calm or cause for alarm
Chanukah strikes a note that touches us all.

Miracles took place in times long gone
When oil for one day burned for eight
And the Maccabees small army struggled on
Led by Judah, a principled man who played it straight,

Winning out over the mightier band
Teaching us courage, the will to succeed.
Perseverance, determination, then and now have saved our land,
Given us hope and a noble creed.

We celebrate these miracles every year without end.
We light candles in our menorahs each evening, eight days.
It is our joyous holiday with family and friends.
We thank God for seeing us to another year and sing his praise.

June 19, 2000

The Joys Of Chanukah,
Our Festival Of Lights

Oh Menorah, how brightly you burn!
    What a glow you cast, in the room
        and in our hearts, on this last day of Chanukah.
            Eight candles for the eighth day, plus the Shamos.

I remember the candle lighting of my childhood
    orange candles in a ten cent, gold-tinted tin menorah.
        As a gift, we were given a few coins, "Chanukah Gelt".

When we four children married,
    our mother gave each of us a silver menorah,
        all of them the same. For more than fifty years
            we have used them proudly, joyfully, on this holiday.

The only thing that has changed is the candles.
    From the smooth-sided orange, we moved on
        to the multi-colored twisted ones from Israel.

What remains exactly the same is the spirit of the holiday.
    Family gathered round taking turns lighting a candle with
    the Shamos,
        reciting the blessings,
        telling the Chanukah story to our children.

One day they will tell it to their own,
   "Dor L'Dor," Generation To Generation.
      We sing songs, play dreidel games, exchange gifts and
      eat latkes.

It wouldn't be Chanukah without the hot, crispy, potato pancakes
   with applesauce and sour cream.
      No matter how many we make, they all vanish.
      "Chag Sameach," Happy Chanukah to one and all.

June 12, 2000

Courage To Continue Writing

How does one write something exciting when what is being written is commonplace? Why would anyone want to read my story when their own may be far more interesting? Someone once said of something totally unrelated, "It may not be much, but it's mine."

So, I will continue to write my memories intermingled with poems, short stories, observations, thoughts, and allow the readers to draw their own conclusions. Could be what I think is nothing unusual, ordinary, my readers may find very different from their own experience, from their own frame of reference and this gives me courage to continue writing.

December 17, 1997

Bailando Sola

Spanish Version

La musica suena
Bailo por la sala
Nadie me ve, estoy sola
Es triste, si, muy triste estar sola.

Me encanta la musica,
Tengo que bailar cuando siento el ritmo
Pero no hay nadie con quien bailar,
Por eso bailo sola, siempre sola.

Dancing Alone

English Version

The music plays
I dance around the living room,
No one sees me. I am alone
It is sad, yes, very sad to be alone.

The music enchants me
I have to dance, when I feel the rhythm
But there is no one to dance with me,
So I dance alone, always alone.

Valentines Day

Once, Valentines Day meant I would receive
    A RED satin heart shaped box of chocolates
       Or a bouquet of RED carnations or
            a RED garnet pin and lots of kisses.

Valentine cards came every year through fifty years of
marriage and five before. One, so ugly, held for me some
special kind of fascination, a silly male character on the front,
pulling a long wad of chewing gum out of his mouth, the
sentiment says, *"I want you for my sweetie, by gum"*.

Today, on this rainy Valentines Day,
    In remembrance of happier ones past,
        I wear a RED velvet robe, RED slippers and RED
        garnet pin.
        I pour a glass of RED wine and drink a toast to him.

February 14, 1998

Thoughts

Beyond The Mist

Driving north from Santa Cruz, along the Coast Road, an ethereal mist rolls in from the Pacific. It filters through the Cypress Trees wending its way eastward. Soon the skyline of San Francisco rises from beyond the mist.

July 1997

A Low-lying Cloud

A low-lying cloud wafts around the mountain like a white chiffon scarf wrapped around my neck and slung over my shoulder, while driving to school on a misty morning.

Written in 1985

Creativity

I believe that I have a creative bent, but I am getting old, and I don't know how far I can go with it, in the time I have left. I will keep plodding on.

If nothing comes of it in this life then perhaps in my next life (if there is an afterlife) I will further my talents.

February 11, 1997

Red Wine

I sip the sweet red wine,
Soft, like a kiss on my lips.

Like silk, it glides down my throat.
Its warmth radiates in my chest.
And throughout my body.

Calmness settles in and waves away
The longings of this Valentine's Day.

February 14, 1998

Water

Left to Nature in its pristine state
WATER: clear, clean, pure
Necessary as air
The way God intended it to be

Man invades, uses, abuses
WATER: dirty, slimy, polluted
Shameful our apathy
Our life's blood defiled.

October 6, 2000

That Time Again

April fifteenth
    deadline to file
        approaching fast

Resent the time
    energy spent
        gathering data

There must be
    less stressful ways
        to pay taxes

Wish I could
    figure out
        HOW?

March 7, 1998

Whispered Words

Secrets told in whispers,
Whispered words, oh yes!
The sort dreams are made of,
The kind lives are built on.

Love poems whispered,
The best kind, the dearest kind,
The most meaningful kind,
Soft, sweet, endearing.

What pleasure in these declarations,
Meant only for two, a unique involvement,
Shared confidentially between soul-mates,
Quiet exhilaration, hearts palpitation, tingling
sensation.

One who has not experienced such an intimate
interchange,
Cannot appreciate those whispered words.
Words of special meaning like no other, given and
received,
Saved up for just the right time for telling.

Acknowledging, understanding, agreeing,
Unquestioning, knowing without doubt,
The joy of loving another, the greatest love knowable,
And I have known such a love.

November 3, 2002

The Train Ride Home

How pleasant the three hour train ride is today.
Normally boring, shaking rattling as it rolls along from Los
Angeles to San Diego.
Puffy white clouds in a Cerulean blue sky, endless calm sea,
with hardly a ripple.

Green hills now separate the train from the sea.
Wildflowers, outcroppings, exposing sedimentation layers,
A feast for my painter's eyes and receptive heart.

I have come this way before when the trip dragged on and on
And I couldn't wait to get to my destination.
Why is it that this day, what I see has grabbed and held my attention.

Lifting my spirits to fly away with the seabirds,
I begin to write about what I see
And what I feel, and before I know it,

I hear the conductor call out
"San Diego",
And I am home.

April 14, 1998

Somebody's Hands

Somebody's hands shoveled
All this sand from off the tracks.
Not just one somebody,
But the hands of many.

The train has stopped.
I admire the now tranquil scene.
The sand, heaped high beside the tracks
Speaks of this past winter's storms.

I gaze as the frothy gentle waters
Roll on to what is left
Of a beach that once must have been
Much wider.

Before crazed El Nino with it's gone mad tides
Scooped up all this sand from the beach
And hurled it onto the tracks
Which then had to be removed, by somebody's hands.

April 14, 1998

Overheard

One speaks of beer:
> "Bud's the best." "No, Coors."
> "See how much I can drink!"
> "Let's have a beer." Chug-a lug

One speaks of hair:
> "Can't do anything with it."
> "Too kinky! Must be straightened."
> "Too straight! Need a perm."
> "Have to wash it, dry it, dye it, curl it."

What about the homeless, the sick, the hungry?
> Tragedies left and right.
> So many in trouble.
> So many in need.

Beer?   Hair?
> Why don't they get their priorities straight?
> Why don't they really do something worthwhile?
> Forget the beer – Volunteer!
> Forget the hair – Share!

May 10, 1998

Hi Handsome!

Are you looking over your shoulder,
Wondering who I might be addressing
Wondering if it might possibly be you?
Could be, maybe,
Then again, maybe not.

Handsome? That depends!
Clark Gable you're not,
Even you, have to agree.
But, would Clark Gable have given
A second glance at me?

October 8, 2000

It's Over

Once upon a time when youth was mine
And all that I've become was yet to be,
I reveled in the joy of then and there
And looked ahead, to future possibility.

We played and romped on beaches and in fields.
We frolicked, fluttered with the butterflies.
Summer passed. I'm left alone,
To lick my wounds, mid salty tears and sighs.

July 24, 1998

Don't Make Promises You Can't Keep

Every time I think this is the last time
I'll do this,
      go there
          say that.

After a while, I find myself
doing this
      going there
          saying that.

So, anytime in the future
That I find myself about to
      do this
          go there
              say that.

I'll stop agonizing and just do it!!!

July 1997

My Three Friends

Three Bs spell...SECURITY

1. "B" – binky (a pacifier)
2. "Baba"- bottle
3. "Bankie" – blanket

When it's naptime or bedtime, I cannot go to my crib without all three friends. With B in one hand and Baba in the other, my eyes are heavy as Mommy carries me to my room. I plaintively call for my Bankie.

Grandma crocheted this Bankie to fit my brother's bassinet when he was born six years ago. It was packed away after he outgrew it. When I came along, it became mine. It is white and pale blue, and oh so soft.

As we head for my bed, I hold it to my cheek. How I love the feel of it. In Grandma's house, when I am tired I climb onto Grampa's big leather chair with my three Bs.

If my brother hurts my feelings or I hurt his, and Mommy scolds me, I want my three Bs. I lie down on the carpet, cuddle Bankie, and I am comforted.

Wherever I go, I take Bankie with me and the two other Bs are close-by. My little fingers fit neatly between the stitches, so that as I walk, Bankie slung over my right shoulder trails along behind me.

Grandma watches me with a smile on her face and says, "I don't know when I have given a gift that was more loved."

August 15, 1998

Reprieve

Early Monday morning I begin the walk to the school where I teach, just around the corner from my house. I hear the crisp crunch of my booted footsteps on the crust of ice that the cold of night has formed over yesterday's fallen snow.

I watched the snowflakes fall gently all day Sunday. They piled up, one upon the other slowly, steadily mounting on the Dogwoods that line our street and on the big old Pine beside the kitchen door, branches weighted down.

Now as I start down the driveway, I listen to the stillness, but hear only the crunch of my steps breaking through the icy cover and see my boots sink through the soft snow beneath, up to mid-calf. I stop, retrace my steps, shake off loose snow,
> go back inside,
>> turn on the radio and hear
>>> "All schools will be closed today."

December 26, 1998

Another Ride Home

Once I ended a story thus: "Want to make a three hour train-ride go by fast? Then start writing!" Again, I am on the train, returning from Los Angeles to San Diego. One hour of the three hour trip has gone by - slowly - much too slowly. Two more hours to go, shaking and rattling, Oh No! I take pen and pad from my purse and begin to write.

The conductor has just announced, "San Juan Capistrano". Jerk!! Not the conductor, but the train. I look out the window and behind red-tile roofs; I admire the mountains in the background. Now, I see Surfside Inn and a whole line of inns, one after the other. I turn to see what is opposite them. It's the Pacific! It is not blue at all, and the reason is that the sky is overcast. The sea reflects the sky. Even so, sun filters through and shines on the water. I change my seat to the right side of the aisle so that I can see the ocean better. It is December fifth and there are some hardy souls out there in the water. Looking southwest at the horizon, the sky is misty grey and the sea a deeper misty grey. It is hard to see where they meet. Directly west the sun blinds my eyes. I squint and from the train, as far out as my eyes can take me; I see the silver path of the sun on the water. The Coast Highway has somehow crept in between me and the ocean. Now, lagoons come into view and water fowl, a marina with lots of boats moored. A few more jerks and we have come to a stop in…damned if I know. No signs, no announcement when the conductor passes on my left and quietly says, "Solana Beach, next. Did you move ma'am?" "Yes, I did from there", I point. He moves my ticket from there to here and continues on down the aisle. It is quiet on the train today, unlike the day before Thanksgiving when I rode in the opposite direction. That day the train was jam-packed with people, standing all the way to L.A., and holding on to the overhead metal rail. When I boarded where the train sets out from in San Diego, already the train was full. I was lucky to get the last empty seat but no window to see out and the people were noisy in the holiday mood. I would not have been able to write even if I wanted to. We have not yet reached Solana Beach, had to stop to let a northbound train go by.

We are on our way again and are coming into Solana Beach. An hour has passed since I started to write. My eyes haven't wanted to close as they did during the first hour of this trip while I worked on a crossword puzzle. They have been too busy watching and observing, I have been writing down what they have been seeing. Each time I ride this train, I write. You would think I have said it all and seen all there is to see and yet there is always something new, something different, and no two of my train writings have ever been the same. Today for the first time, I have looked out several times and found that we were riding through eroded cliffs on both sides. Why have I never noticed this before?

The three hour train ride is ending. The sky is showing larger areas of blue now. It appears to be welcoming me home as we approach San Diego.

December 5, 1999

The Voice Of Silence

Yes, silence has a voice that speaks to me.
At times, it is unwelcome.
It points out to me how lonely I am.
In order to avoid listening to its voice,
I keep the radio on all day so that I don't
have to hear the silence.

Other times, silence is welcome.
It speaks to me of peace and serenity.

Noise, talk, too many words,
too many conflicting opinions, idle chatter,
my head feels as if it is about to explode.
Then the silence says, "Relax, appreciate,
enjoy me, be calm," and I listen to its voice,
and revel in it.

December 14, 1998

Then And Now

Then:

There was World War II. We were young,
He said, "If I come back, we will take up
Where we left off". He enlisted in the Army.
Time dragged it's feet. His four years of service
Seemed endless.

He did come back, and soon after, we married.
We raised our two children, worked hard and
Pulled together. Our days were full, busy,
So much so, that we were unaware how the years,
One after another, slipped by.

The day came when our children surprised
Us with a beautiful party to celebrate
Our Fiftieth Wedding Anniversary.
Five months later he died.

Now:

No more meeting schedules of someone else's needs.
No one to account to, answer to, explain to
    Ever since he died,
    Ever since I have been alone,
    I am drifting...

Not wanting to see people,
Not wanting to make the effort to talk
Or go for a walk, or write, or paint, or sew, or create.
For the time being I have set aside my "Joie de Vivre".

Alone, I sit on the lawn, pulling weeds and crabgrass.
More will grow.
Alone, I climb up on our hill, picking up twigs and
leaves. More will fall,
Useless pursuits, these…as if I could hold back Natures
Plan,
Anymore than I could hold back death.

August 25,1997

What Are The Odds

Maybe once if we're lucky
Maybe once we will find
All wrapped up in one person
That perfect meeting of minds.

How rare such a treasure!
What are the odds?

Who among us hasn't dreamt
Of finding the   "RIGHT" one?
Is it fantasy to dream?
What do we settle for
In the real world we live in?

October 12, 2000

A Birthday Present

October came and with it, Alexander's seventh and Joshua's second birthdays. What will I get them? I had no idea.

I happened to be in Costco's one day, and on an end display I saw some fluffy throws. I thought: What a good idea! These will be great to lie on or wrap around themselves while sitting on the floor watching T.V.

I selected one with a black background and jewel colored triangles and diamonds for Alex. For Joshua, I picked a beige background with Southwestern designs. I could picture the two of them in front of the T.V. cuddled snugly in their blankets.

Alex loved his on sight. He immediately spread it out on the floor, and lay down on it: His left hand cupped under his chin, his right hand rubbing the blanket from side to side, he said: "Grandma, I'm glad you got this for me. I really like it." When he went to bed, he insisted on taking it with him.

Joshua, on the other hand, looked at it indifferently and went for his Bankie, the one I had crocheted and which he loves so much. Oh well, one of these days when he has outgrown Bankie and the baby stage, he may discover the replacement and find it is more appropriate for a growing boy.

November 13, 1998

2001 Valentine

Beautiful people
Kind and good
Loving and caring

    At this season
    Of Red satin hearts
    Fragrant red flowers

Tiny candy hearts
With sentimental sayings
Cupids' arrows aiming

    On this special day
    Set aside for showing
    And telling one another

I say to you:
"I love you,
Happy Valentines Day."

February 14, 2001

From My Pen

Partially written stories,
    A word or phrase I heard,
Or, one I conjured up,
    And quickly jotted down,
On a scrap of paper, or envelope,
    Or newspaper on the counter,
Waiting to be read.
    Lest I forget it, and it flies away.

Someday, yes someday,
    I will complete that story.
Use that word or phrase.
    Weave it into something
Wonderful or profound.
    Or, less than wonderful,
Maybe not even good.
    But, it may touch someone.
Turn his life around.
    Miracles happen, so they say.

October 2, 1998

A Sonata

Musical poetry
Poetic music
Both intertwine
Twist together, like a rope.

Beautiful music is poetic.
Poetry well written is musical.
A Sonata

February 26, 2001

Expanding My Mind

I'm surfing the dictionary, not the web.
Finding words I never knew,
Words that catch my eye,
Words that energize me,
Words that pique my interest.

I read their meanings
And learn and grow.

Summer of 1999

A Limerick

There once was a gal from Santee,
Who had a pain in her knee.
And her back ached besides,
In and out like the tides.
"Guess I'll go for a walk", said she.

"A walk when you're sore?" you ask.
"Are you sure you are up to the task?"
There's no sense in crying,
Pain's there, no denying.
"If it hurts, I'll just put on a mask."

March 17, 1999

Phyllis

I cry as I write, thinking about my loss.
My only sister, who went so fast, left too soon.

Almost a year has passed and I cannot adjust to life
without her.
Nor can I accept that she is dead.

I want to call her, tell her a bit of news.
I want her to see my new house.

I need her advice, her input, but there is no way I can get it!
Not from her, not anymore.

I am angry with her for leaving me to fend for myself,
Leaving me alone, deserting me.

She was the baby, the little one.
She looked up to me.

The tables turned, then I needed her and I need her now.
And she is nowhere to be found.

What good is my crying? What good are my tears?
My sister is gone.

February 5, 2002

Cream Cheese

"Cream Cheese," the newest addition to our family, is a Blue Point Himalayan Kitten. My grandson, Alexander, gave him the name. This feline, creamy in color, has blue eyes, blue-tipped ears, paws and tail. "Roquefort would be a better name," said Anita, his mom, but Alexander prevailed and "Cream Cheese" it remains.

Anita tells me that he is frisky and playful. When she opens the door of the dishwasher, he is inside in a flash. One of these days, if she isn't careful, she'll have a washed and dried kitten, providing he survives the ordeal...Heaven forbid! I shudder at the thought. When I told this to my neighbor, she said, "When Patches was a kitten, I turned on the clothes dryer and heard "thump, thump'. I quickly opened the door and out jumped Patches, stunned, but none the worse for wear." Anita also told me that when she opens the doors of the side-by-side refrigerator/freezer, the kitten jumps in. She knows enough to be watchful and hopefully Alexander will be careful too or else he'll turn into a frozen Cream Cheese. After the disappearance recently of "Goldilocks", their Persian cat, I dread to think what may happen to Cream Cheese at the rate he's going.

I am to meet the little terror this coming weekend. Although I am a softy for a tiny ball of fluff, I am apprehensive about having him in my house. Alexander has assured me that his claws will be cut before they bring him so that he doesn't claw my furniture. "I promise you Grandma, he will not poop or wet on your carpet. He goes in his box."

Anita called today to say she had a bad night and very little sleep. "Last night", she said, "as I was preparing to go to bed and started to turn out the lights, I realized that Cream Cheese wasn't around. Jeff and I searched the house. No kitty! We called, no response!" Flashlights in hand, they looked under bushes in the back yard, though the kitten had never been outdoors. Back inside, they looked in closets, cupboards, and garage…nothing! Anita began to cry. Visions of Goldilocks mysterious disappearance filled her mind. "I can't deal with this anymore tonight. I'll have a glass of milk, go to bed, and see what happens in the morning." As she opened the refrigerator door, Cream Cheese came leaping up to her. She called me the next morning. "Mom, I had no idea where the kitten was hiding but then I reasoned that there is a narrow space between the TV cabinet and the wall, just enough for the kitten to wiggle through onto a shelf behind the VCR".

On Sunday, Anita arrived in her van with her two children, Cream Cheese, and all their bags and baggage. Cream Cheese's carrier was placed under the buffet in the dining room. His litter box was set on the tile floor in the front entry hall. Beside it a mat with a bowl of water and a bowl of food. He immediately settled in and took over. "Just see", I said, "he is right at home here, acting like King of the Hill."

"He has more places to sit in your house, Grandma, than at home," Alex noted. During the week, before I sat in my chair, I checked first because quite often I found him sleeping there. Of course, Alex's parents hadn't gotten around to having his claws trimmed before they left home and after they left my house, I found that the little ball of fluff did a good job of shredding my bedroom curtains. Needless to say Cream Cheese wasn't invited back.

1999

113

A Lot of Days, A Lot of Living

Eighteen thousand four hundred days.
How could we know when we said, "I do",
If it would last, or would we go our own ways?
That's just the point, we had no clue.

There had to be something to make us hold fast.
Through good times and bad. Oh we had our share.
But we respected our commitment to make it last
And all because we really did care.

Fifty years plus five months more.
That's what all those days added up to be.
What a lot of living; not a bad score,
That is when you were taken from me.

Now it's just "I"…… no longer "We".

April 15, 2002

Life Begins At Forty

Who says, "Life begins at forty?"
Yeah! Sure! It begins to go downhill.
No matter how we try to avoid it.
We grow old against our will.

August 13, 1997

It's A Paper World

Papers, papers inundation
How to go through it all, saturation
Letters to read, bills to be paid
Junk to toss out, lists to be made
Things to be filed, others to store
When I think I am finished, along comes more.

February 2, 1997

Moon

Oh, moon, so far away,
shining your silvery path
down on me, as I stand
on my patio, admiring you.

All those stars
twinkling round you
sparkling, light up
the nighttime sky.

This mild soft night
wraps its arms around me,
embracing me like a lover.
This is truly heaven sent.

Surrounded by your light,
bathed in its loveliness
so pure and clear,
I feel cleansed and, oh, so vulnerable.

July 14, 2002

Love

Nothing equals the ecstasy of love.
What can compare to being "In Love"?
I come up with only one answer.
Love that comes with a child's arrival.

Each love is powerful in its own way.
The significant other in your life may come or go,
But your child is your child, always.
Yet, children grow up, and sometimes leave you.

If two people together, weather all the tests,
The ups and downs, joys and heartaches,
Advances and setbacks, hopes and disappointments,
All that life and living bring.

Even if children should go,
If they survive all of that,
Then perhaps that love is,
The strongest love, after all.

10 Commandments

1. Be cheerful, smile.
   No one wants to be in the company of a Sourpuss.

2. Look your best at all times.
   No one appreciates a sloppy appearance. It pulls them down, as well as yourself.

3. Eat sensibly and well.
   T.V. dinners and fast foods are not good for you.

4. You must get out.
   See a show, movie, or concert. Do things that make you feel good. Do not mope around the house.

5. Be creative.
   Indulge in the arts in some manner. Paint a picture, write a story, cook something interesting, decorate your home, arrange flowers, or decorate a platter. If none of these things are appealing, try a coloring book and crayons.

6. Listen to the news, read.
   Be aware of what is going on around the world, so that you can talk about current events.

7. Do not talk about your aches and ailments.
   Everyone has their own and they don't need the burden of carrying yours around as well.

8. Make someone laugh.
   There is more than enough of a serious nature going on around us. Give someone, including yourself, a lift.

9. Pay someone a compliment.
   Not only will it make that person feel good, but you will feel good too, for having done it.

10. Call or write someone.
    Tell them how often you think of them and how you miss them. Remind them of something pleasant that you shared in the past. Go on make their day!

April 15, 2002

Another Valentines Day

Valentines Day is coming soon,
Reminding me of others shared,
When love was young in full bloom,
And hearts and thoughts were bared.

We looked ahead to more of them,
Thinking time was infinite.
We felt so invincible then,
Nothing could put an end to it.

How wrong we were, how innocent,
To think along eternal lines
Presuming we'd go on together,
Until, the end of time.

A power, stronger than we two combined,
Determined which of us would stay.
So, here I sit alone, deploring fate.
It's just another Valentines Day.

Mignon

In the early 1950's my husband and I were walking one day along Main St., in Port Washington, NY, the town in which we lived. As we passed by a shop we noticed a heavy statuette sitting on the floor holding the front door open. We stopped and walked closer to the door. The figure was very dark, almost black. We wondered whether it had been painted over or perhaps it had darkened with age. It appeared to be an old piece. We bent down to look at it more closely. I was intrigued by the beautiful face of the woman. In front of the base we could see some letters but couldn't make out what it said.

Something about that figure drew us into the store. My husband said, "I'm curious about that statue on the floor by the front door. What's it made of?"

"Oh, it's just white metal."

"How much do you want for it?"

He thought for a moment, "twenty –five dollars" he answered.

My husband walked back to the doorway. He squatted, tilted the figure back, noted it was hollow with thick walls. He took a key from his pocket and put a scratch on the inside. He saw immediately that this was not white metal but a gold colored metal of some kind. "We'll take it" he said as he paid the man. I waited while he went to bring the car. He had all he could do to lift the figure by its arms and carry it out to the back of our station wagon.

It took a lot of rubbing and polishing on my part, over a long period of time working in stages, to get the black off and the bronze figure back to its rightful luster and beauty. The letters which were illegible at the time of purchase when finally cleared of all the grime, spelled the name Mignon. She is Mignon, the gypsy girl of the opera Mignon. She is seated on a bench and propped up against the side of the bench by her leg is a musical instrument which appears to be a lute. The figure is twenty-one inches high; the base is twelve inches deep by ten inches wide. It is a substantial piece.

My husband and I knew we had a valuable thing when the name of the artist appeared on the right side of the base. It says: E. AIZELIN 1880 carved in ¼ inch high letters. On the left side it says: F. BARBEDIENNE, FONDEUR, PARIS. This is the foundry where the bronze figure was cast.

When Mignon was cleaned and polished, I decided to have it electrified and made into a lamp. We took it to a shop in Manhasset, which was recommended to us. The proprietor offered us sixty dollars for it. Silly man! No way would we sell our treasure. We reasoned, if he offered this amount, no doubt he'll sell it at a handsome profit. We had him electrify it, and when it was ready, we brought Mignon home, where she has graced my home for over fifty years.

At that time, we kept Mignon in our bedroom, atop a black cherry chest. When my nephew Harry was a little boy, about three, he would tap on my bedroom door and ask to see the beautiful lady."

Whenever we refer to the statue we call her by her name. For example, Mignon needs to be polished or Mignon needs a new lampshade.

I have never taken Mignon to be appraised. Putting a dollar value on something I truly treasure couldn't possibly make me appreciate her more. I'll leave that for my daughter to do at some future time, if she so desires.

June 10, 2002

Crystal Chandelier

Tinkling crystals, respond to a breeze.
Ping, ping, as if tapped by a fingernail.
One gently touches another like wind chimes.

Sparkling crystals reflect the lights.
Glint, glint, as a shaft touches a facet.
Sending out myriads of rainbows.

Teardrop crystals and oval shapes, like droplets
Drip, drip, dripping from a waterfall.
Ping, glint, drip, glowing,

Enveloping the room by its beauty.

Uplifted

There'll be no cloud hanging over my head.
I'll be dancing on that cloud instead.
I refuse to let anything get me down.
When a negative shows up, I say, "Get out of town,

Go on, disappear! I've no time for you."
There are too many fun things I have to do.
Life is too short, make the most of today.
Can't wait for tomorrow. I'll show you the way.

Just climb up on that cloud and don't look down.
Sing, be merry, laugh like a clown.
You'll feel better, others round you will too,
If they learn this lesson, that's what they'll do.

And won't this crazy world be a happier place,
When we're all up there dancing, face to face.

October 4, 2002

Rabbits, Damn It!

Rabbits have bad habits.
They multiply too fast,
For people who care about their lawns and gardens,
And resent the invasion destruction.

I no longer think kindly of the critters,
As I look at my ruined back yard,
And see their pellets all over,
What used to be soft, green grass.

The cute little white tailed bunnies,
Appear to be happy campers,
As they scamper up my hill. Or, was it their hill,
 Before we invaded their land?

The Invasion

One night, in the dark, I missed the left turn into my street. As I realized I had passed it, my headlights startled a lot of rabbits in the road. They took off across the lawns on my left and I presume on up the hill behind the houses. My house is at the base of the same hill.

I have talked to the neighbors on either side of my house. One has very little growth on his hill, thanks to the rabbits. The other just had a chain link fence installed at the top of his hill.

"It won't help", I told him, "see where they come under my fence". In a day or two sure enough, you could see their path under the gate of his new fence. He gathered some rocks and placed them in that spot, but the next day, the brazen bunnies had pushed the rocks aside. Next, he put up chicken wire on the outside of his fence, hoping that would solve the problem.

Driving home today, along Mast Blvd., just over a roof, on my right, I saw a big bird with a wide wingspread. I never before saw such a bird so close. Eagle? Hawk? "Yes, it must be a hawk", I reasoned. From its talons hung what I took to be a rabbit.

On the top of the hill behind my house, there has lived for a number of years, a pair of hawks. We have watched them soaring.

For several months now, rabbits have taken over my hill. If they kept to the hill, that would be fine, but when they come down and under my fence, then on down into my yard, this makes me angry. My green lawn has been stripped bare. Rabbit pellets have replaced the green. They have consumed the contents of the planters on the patios as well as most plants in the raised bed.

I asked my neighbor three houses down if these terrorists bothered him. He said, "No, not the way my yard is set up, with walls and the swimming pool". I showed him what became of my yard. I told him, "this is no longer the isolated visit, and they are coming down in numbers".

"Well, you know, rabbits love rabbits" he said, "And since the hawks left, they are multiplying". I didn't realize that the hawks had gone, though about a week ago I thought I saw one flying over my hill.

Recently, my daughter and her family visited me. One morning I went out back and saw a dead mutilated animal. I called to my kids, "Come see"! They came out. It was a decapitated rabbit. My son-in-law got a shovel, I a plastic bag; rabbit in bag, tied with a twistem, my son-in-law transported it to a public dumpster where he deposited it. Last week I found another in the same spot.

Seeing the big bird today, with its prey, I felt encouraged. "One more out of the way", I thought "Maybe the hawks will eliminate this recent plague".

I wish those dear birds the best. I hope they have a feast.

Sequel To The Rabbit Saga

I'm so happy today, let me tell you why. The hawks are back! I pulled back the curtains on this gray day, looked to the top of the hill and saw a hawk circling. Round and round it soared. When it came over my yard, its wings spread wide, I thought "Ah, Good! Now those rabbits surely will be gone. But where is the other hawk, its mate?

I stood by the patio door admiring the grace of that majestic bird as it dipped and rose, circling, circling. Off to the east, I noticed a bird coming in this direction. As it approached, I realized it was the other hawk. It came to rest for just a minute or two on top of a pole, then joined its mate, circling over my hill.

Welcome back birds, good to see ya! Bye, bye, bunnies.

Scary, Scary Night

Scary, Scary Night
Ghosts and goblins clad in white
Bugs and spiders and cobwebs galore
Weird Jack O'Lanterns surround the front door.

Plastic pumpkins, pillowcases, trick or treat bags
Just toss in the treats for the witches and hags
An endless parade of vampires and bats
Owls, ravens, scorpions and green-eyed cats.

Draculas, Frankensteins, skeletons and tramps
Turn the corner, round the bend, up and down ramps
Costumes of scarecrows, monsters, trolls and elves
Made by parents or the kids themselves

Painted faces, wigs, masks, teeth with fangs
Some come with a parent, others in gangs
But it's all in the spirit of good clean fun
Enjoyed by the givers, receivers, everyone.

Candy's all gone, lights turned off, doors are shut
As the beggars turn homeward to count their loot
And off in the distance you can hear someone call,
"Happy Halloween and a Scary, Scary Night to All."

October 13, 2002

Relax

Too often we are so involved
    meeting schedules
        watching the clock.

All of us need to seize the time
    to laze on the grass
        look up at the sky

study the clouds, their shapes, formations
    equate them with this animal or that
        allow our cares to drift away …away

or, sit on the sand
    let it sift through our fingers
as we gaze out to sea.
    think private thoughts
or don't think at all
    breathe the salt air
welcome the fresh breezes
    that come in off the ocean to greet us.

Ah… blissful peace, so rare.

An Angel On My Shoulder

Mama said, "No, you cannot go to the movies with Gloria and Vincent". I decided to walk the few blocks with them and then come on home. As I walked back, a man approached me. I can picture this man still. I can see him as clearly as if this happened yesterday. He was a man in his sixties, swarthy, perhaps five feet eight inches tall, stocky build. He wore a pair of dark pants, a striped shirt with long sleeves, no tie, wide suspenders and a Panama straw hat. He told me he had a granddaughter just my size. He said he bought a dress for her and asked me if I would try it on so that he could see if it was the right size for her.

Today, knowing what we do, we warn our children about talking to strangers. I don't ever remember my parents telling me about such things. Being an innocent little girl, nine or ten years old, I agreed to go with him.

We walked along DeKalb Avenue, two blocks to Tompkins Avenue and turned left. It was a long walk to Moore Street, perhaps twenty blocks. I remember asking him several times how much further it was. Each time he said we would be there soon and he would talk to me, to distract me, I realize now. We also stopped to look in the store windows along Tompkins Avenue, a business street. When we came to Moore Street, we turned left. The left side of that block was lined with white tenements. At one of the buildings, we walked up several steps to the double door entry.

Just at that moment, I stopped. "My mother will be looking for me", and as I was saying it, I turned, dashed down those steps and ran all the way home.

I have to believe that an angel was watching over me. Why else would I have innocently walked with this man and then at that very moment, turned and ran? The man did not chase me. It would have attracted too much attention to see an old man chasing a little girl. As I ran, I thought, "If I just walked to the movies, I should have been back soon. Will Mama and Daddy be worried? Will they be looking for me? Will they be angry?"

When I reached home, I don't remember telling my parents what happened, perhaps because I was afraid they would yell at me for walking to the movie theatre in the first place, and then for going somewhere with a stranger. I buried the incident.

I cannot remember exactly when or why I retrieved the incident. One day, not too many years ago, I found myself telling it to my husband. After that, I told it to my daughter and to my sister. I have felt emotional whenever I have told it. As I tell the story, I wonder, "Will it be believed?" It doesn't matter whether it is believed or not. It happened!

I wonder, why did I not remember it until recent years, and when I did, why is it so clear in my mind? I wonder too, why is it so upsetting to me now after all this time? Is it because knowing what I do now, I realize what could have happened to me that day so long ago?

Statistics now show that the age for young girls who are abducted and molested is nine to ten years old. That is exactly how old I was. Thank you for protecting me, my Guardian Angel!

After I wrote this story, I became curious to see a map of Brooklyn, New York. I wanted to retrace the walk I took with that man. I had estimated that we walked twenty blocks, almost seventy years ago. I wrote to the Brooklyn Borough Hall and received from them detailed maps of that era. Sure enough, I found Moore Street and the route we walked. It was nineteen blocks.

June 15, 1997

Tell Me

Tell me once again,
Tell me evermore,
Tell me now and then,
As you never have before.

Tell me while you can,
Tell me while I'm here,
Tell me like the man,
I know you are, My Dear.

Tell me it's for always,
Tell me it's no game,
Tell me it's for all our days,
And I will do the same.

Take A Break

I think I'll have a cup of tea.
Right now, this sounds good to me.
It's cold outside and I've just come in.
A few minutes break won't be a sin

Before I get started doing my chores,
Besides, it will warm me clear through to my pores.
I must run uptown, get a few errands done,
Then hurry on home to make dinner. What fun!

My son will come home and my daughter and spouse.
I have to do laundry and tend to the house.
Ah! The water is boiling. Now I'll fix the tea
And take these few minutes, just for me.

1975

Gypsy

It's a moonlit night in Romany.

Gypsy wagons encircle a blazing fire.

The men pick up their mandolins and slowly begin to strum.

One starts the song and one by one the others join in, "Zegeune, Zegeune".

A gypsy woman rises and begins to dance, tapping her tambourine.

Another joins her and yet another, until all the women are dancing around the fire.

Their skirts twirling, swirling as the music gains momentum.

They spin and spin in a frenzy.

The fire fades, the musicians slow down, and so too the dancers.

Only embers remain, as the couples pair off and stroll to their wagons.

Who Am I

I am the color of Rudolph's nose.
I'm Santa's suit and ribbon bows.
I'm the Christmas color most often in use
And also the color of cranberry juice.

I'm up at the corner, on a sign that says "stop".
I'm lollypops, Jell-O and soda pop.
I am the cherry they put on top
Of a gooey sundae in an ice cream shop.

I'm tomato soup, spaghetti sauce,
Ketchup and pomegranates and of course
A hot dog, a hamburger before it's been cooked.
I'm stuffed in an olive and then overlooked.

I'm a jelly apple, a currant, a radish, a beet.
A shade that is definitely not discreet,
I am a color you're likely to meet
When you're very angry and filled with heat.

I'm the proud hair on some people's heads.
I'm rubies and garnets and wintertime sleds.
I'm lipstick, I'm rouge, I'm painted nails.
I'm the sunset's reflection on sailboat's sails.

I'm brilliant and beaming and bursting and bright
Like the summer sun when it's reached its full height.
I'm fierce, I'm fiery, I'm very exciting,
Like the tempers of people when they are fighting.

I'm not a color to be quiet about.
I am a color to make you shout out.
I'm the sound of a siren, a trumpet, a scream,
When you waken at night from a frightening dream.

I'm a firecracker, a fire alarm,
The stripes on our flag, a barn on a farm.
I'm the tip of a match and the part of a flame
That makes you wonder from whence I came.

I'm an apple for teacher, a ladybug creature
A clown's round nose, his prominent feature.
A poppy, a tulip, a fragrant rose,
I'm also the color of loads of clothes.

I'm a cardinal's feathers, a robin's breast
And the failing marks on your spelling test.
In a deck of cards, I'm the diamonds and hearts.
I'm the deliciousness of strawberry tarts.

A puzzling thought just entered my mind
Of how my absence would be missed
If I were not added to colors of other kinds,
Purple, orange and pink would not exist.

I'm the stripes on a peppermint candy cane.
I'm the color that can often drive you insane.
I'm half the checkers in a checkerboard game.
Now do you suppose you can guess my name?

1997

The Move

After his open-heart surgery in 1982, my husband was more determined than ever to get away from New York. Jerry wanted to move to a warmer climate. He felt there was nothing to keep him in New York any longer.

Harry and Lou, his two older brothers, had gone to New York years before. They were settled, married young men, working and raising families when, at age sixteen, Jerry felt it was time for him to go to the big city. He went to live with Lou, Ce, and their little boy. Another brother, Dave who was two years younger than Jerry, joined him soon after. Both boys worked, contributed, sent money home to the family in Toronto and continued to live with Lou and Ce until they enlisted in the army, when World War II was declared. Dave was sent to a base in Fresno, California, then, served in the Pacific Theatre. After the war, he married and settled in Fresno.

Jerry and I had met several years before the war. We talked about marriage but because of the uncertainties, decided it would be wiser to wait. He said, "If I come back, we will take up where we left off." He served in Europe…and we waited. He came home in November 1945 and six months later, on May 19, 1946 we were married. We remained in New York, moving from Brooklyn to Port Washington, Long Island, two years later. We lived in that beautiful town for thirty-five years, from 1948 to 1983 when we moved to San Diego, California.

Over the years and until we moved, we lost family members. Jerry's parents died so did Lou and Ce, with whom we were close. Harry and his family had moved to Los Angeles and settled there many years earlier. Of Jerry's family, there were now two brothers in California and a brother Cyril and sister Ethel, with their families remaining in Toronto. He had no one from his family in New York.

I was born in Brooklyn, New York, the second of four children. My father died when I was eighteen during Christmas vacation of my first year at the Traphagen School of Fashion. I had lived nowhere else when I met Jerry. My entire family, immediate and extended, lived in and around New York City. I too suffered the loss of family members, my mother in 1970 and Arthur, my older brother, at fifty-six in 1972. My younger brother, Morton, relocated to Texas with his family. Sister Phyllis married, remained in New York. I had lots of cousins, nieces, nephews, and close friends. New York was my home. I had no desire to ever move from there. Travel? Yes! And we did, as much as time away from business and as much as our finances allowed.

But to leave New York entirely, to relocate, was out of the question. (This is the New York mentality—there is no place to equal New York.) I quote a friend who said, "Everywhere outside of New York City is bucolic". Others claimed, "Leave New York City and you're camping out."

Jerry made up his mind to retire, sell our house, invest the money from the sale and live off the income. I said, "Over my dead body!" I had many reasons for not wanting to go, all valid. I couldn't see parting with my house and moving to an apartment, going to an unknown place, far from where I grew up and what I knew. Leaving my sister and sister-in-law (more a sister to me) and all my family and friends was inconceivable.

Over the years I had been taking college courses, one course a semester in the evening, while working full-time in the school system, working my way up the ladder in this, my second career. When I had accumulated two years of college credits, I became a teacher assistant, working in Special Education. I loved this position; loved working with children with learning disabilities. I was good at what I did and the teachers and principal appreciated me. I had worked so hard to reach this point that I couldn't bear the thought of leaving it. And all the while raising two children, and taking care of my house and home. Sometimes now I wonder how I did it all. No one and nothing suffered as a result of my working and studying. Everything was in order.

In 1982, my son Charles, now 23, was working as an Emergency Medical Technician and had an apartment of his own. My daughter Anita, 18, had graduated from high school and was at this time in Israel for a year, on a work/study program, earning college credits. It was while she was in Israel that we both had our surgeries. We kept it from her not wanting to worry her. We knew that if she found out, she would want to come home to be with us. We both wanted her to finish out her year, and the planned summer of travel in Europe that was to follow.

All the while, Jerry kept working on me about selling the house and moving to California. I fought it. I resisted it. So determined was he to prove his point and get his way that one day he said, "I am going with you or without you." That statement got to me. I saw RED! This was a crucial period in our lives. Not many words were spoken between us for quite some time. I felt like telling him to go. How dare he threaten me this way? I had given too much to this marriage for 35 years, far more than I received from it. If I learned nothing else from all my years of living, I learned that in this world there are givers and takers. Jerry was a taker. He took all that I gave, and expected more.

Look at all I would be giving up: house, family, friends, job. He would be giving up nothing. He would still have me to look after him and his needs and provide for his comfort as I had been doing all along. It took an entire year of wavering, fighting with the thought of uprooting myself, to come to grips with it. It was heart wrenching. Once I made up my mind to go ahead with it, I took charge and handled each phase as it came along. The worst part was making the decision. After that, the rest fell into place, but even that part of it had its bad/sad moments.

We had a big English Tudor house, two floors, full attic, full basement, and two-car garage. We rarely got rid of things. We weren't going anywhere, we had the room, just leave it, it may come in handy sometime…When we bought a new refrigerator, the old one went down to the basement. "Great for drinks, melons, when we have a party"—and we did, lots of them. The next time we got a new one, the old one went into the attached garage. "Great for platters and prepared foods when we entertain." Didn't need baby items like crib, high chair anymore? Put it up in the attic so we'll have it when a baby comes to visit." Got a new mahogany dining room set, the old oak set went down to the basement. The basement and attic became a maze. We had to walk around things to get to other things - but we had it if we needed it and it was all neat and orderly.

Now, as we prepared for moving we had several yard sales and what didn't sell we gave away to members of our family, to teachers I worked with. "Come and take what you can use." My beaver coat went to my niece Gina. My silver fox jacket to my niece Bonnie. I wouldn't need furs in San Diego. Pat Morgan, the music teacher in my school, knew I had many nice things. She said, "What ever you want to sell, Shirley, I will buy for myself and my three daughters." Whatever price I put on the items, she gladly paid without quibbling. In fact, she was so pleased that she invited Jerry and me to their home just before we left, for a farewell dinner. We placed ads in newspapers to sell all the things we couldn't possibly take with us. We sold two automobiles and gave the third, a Chrysler and the best one, to our son. He felt so bad that we were moving away and "deserting him", that whatever he wanted we let him have. The hard part came when I had to decide, "Shall I take it? Shall I sell it? Shall I give it away?"

My silver jewelry workbench with all supplies—sold. So many other things like that. Will I use it? Will I have room for it? Any doubt, sell it! Get rid of it! My garden, my peonies, the pear tree and the big old wild cherry tree in the back yard, all left there.

My neighbors - dear Irish Mary, my rock all these years. Dear Italian Mrs. Nofi with her apron gathered up, bringing me tomatoes, fresh onions, zucchini, and fresh basil from her extensive garden, and figs. These neighbors, friends all the years, can never be replaced or forgotten.

We put the house on the market and with no problem at all, we got what we asked for it.

In June I retired. My principal and staff gave me a wonderful farewell party and presented me with gold lover's knot earrings. That was an emotional evening, saying goodbye to my associates.

I packed some essentials to take with us and in July, Anita and I flew to San Diego. We had a lot to accomplish in a short time. We stayed in a motel that had a furnished unit with kitchen and made ourselves comfortable during an unusual heat wave. We rented a car for a week while we looked for and bought a nice little used car that would become Anita's car for school. We registered her at Grossmont College.

In 1983 San Diego, we could not find an apartment. So, we rented a big beautiful house in San Carlos, the very area I preferred from my earlier trips, and very close to Anita's school. I opened a joint bank account for Jerry and Me, and a checking account for Anita. We bought a leather recliner chair for Jerry, a console TV, a vacuum cleaner, twin beds and bedding and a table. I wanted Anita to be able to function for the month that I would be away. I stocked the pantry, refrigerator and freezer. I hated leaving Anita alone.

Back in Port Washington, we closed on the house. I alone packed 67 cartons. We arranged for the movers and saw to final details. The movers came, loaded the van and took off. We left our valises in the house. Charles picked up Jerry and me and brought us to my sister-in-law's house where we spent the night. The next day he took us back to the house to pick up our luggage. He couldn't bring himself to come inside because he had never seen it empty. Though he continued to live in Port Washington, he never drove down Fairfield Avenue. He took us to Kennedy Airport and left. It was too sad for him to see us go. When we entered the terminal, Debby, my best friend, my maid of honor and her Leo were waiting to see us off.

While I was back East, Anita met Jeff at college. She was not alone much after that. One month to the day after I left, Jerry and I landed at Lindbergh Field in San Diego. Anita and Jeff were there to meet us. (Jeff eventually became our son-in-law.) They drove us to our house on Rondel Court.

Jerry was bug-eyed. He never expected what he saw. I hadn't told him much; I wanted him to be surprised and he was. "When did you buy this chair? What a TV set!" He was impressed. Everything was arranged; made comfortable and easy for "the master".

In a few days our furniture arrived. Within two weeks anyone entering the house would have thought we had been living there for years. We bought a car for ourselves. After putting the house in order, I registered for classes at San Diego State University, made friends, kept up with correspondence (lots of it), gardened and entertained. In that first year, we had fifteen sets of visitors. We took them all on the tour I had laid out, every day another area: coast, inland, mountains, desert, up North, and down to Baja. It didn't take us long to adjust to our new surroundings. We loved the climate and we loved San Diego. Soon after we came, my cousin and her husband came for a trial stay, then, moved here. My sister visited us twice, came to try it for six months and stayed.

I never regretted coming to San Diego. What I do regret is leaving family and friends behind. Some came once or twice to visit. We went back there several times. We call one another, we write, but it is no longer the same. Something is lost when you are not together on a regular basis. This is what I regret and cannot recapture. My two best friends have never seen my grandchildren. This never would have happened had we remained back East.

My niece and nephew, who were like my own children, have never come out here to visit. They were not here when my husband died, but worse still, while he was ailing, one couldn't afford the airfare and the other until recently was afraid to fly. This is what happens when families are separated. They grow apart and this is sad.

That first year, between visitors and various activities, we looked for a house to buy. The rented house was available and at a good price, but it was a big house, up and down stairs, huge rooms-too much to take care of. We knew that Anita would leave before too long and we certainly didn't need such a place for two people. We found a house, all on one level that fit our needs precisely. We bought it and moved in. Two moves in a year and a half. When finally we had everything the way we wanted it, I said, "I don't ever want to move again." Jerry didn't have to; his next move was to his final resting place. He did enjoy this house though, while he was here. We celebrated Anita's graduation with a big party and on every holiday our table was filled with guests all around it. We had many, many happy times here including events centered around Anita's wedding, and later with our grandchildren.

Since Jerry went away and with the passage of time, more and more I realize that I will have to move once again, close to my daughter. And this time it is not Jerry who is putting pressure on me. Anita and her family want me near them. Three hours away is too far in an emergency. Living alone is not the happiest situation either. As before, I am resisting and fighting the inevitable. I know that this next move must take place sooner or later, but I am holding off for as long as I can.

A Poem Evolves

I look outside, another gray day.
I must write something,
But, have nothing to say,
Not at this moment, anyway.

Sandwich in left hand, pen in the right,
I'm eating while listening,
To primary results. Some plight!
Looks like Gore and Bush have begun their fight.

I hate elections, always the same,
One tears down the other.
It's a sad commentary and a shame,
When men with big egos play such a game.

But, a bigger shame when people like me,
Have to settle for someone,
We really don't want and can't see,
Elected our president. Don't you agree?

Dusk

Driving home at end of day
I look, and think and muse
I see the silhouettes of trees
Against the twilight skies
And here and there and in between
The sunset fades and dies.

1957

Mom

Didn't tell you then
Will tell you now
Shall I say, "Wish you were near?
You are and will always be close to my heart.
Love you Mom but I wish you were here."

January 30, 1997

Remembering

Beware of living in the past.
      Reminiscing, telling stories of times long gone.
Others may be bored hearing about
      What used to be.
It matters to us, not to them.
      These were our life experiences, not theirs.
They are building their own memories, which,
      One day will bore the next generation.

Our peers know, understand.
      Some shared the same events with us.
Remembering, we laugh together, cry together.
      Others lived through similar experiences.
We tell, appreciate, each other's long ago stories,
      No fear of boredom from them.
We have gathered our wisdom, paid our dues.
      Made our mistakes, lived.

May 14, 1997

Autumn Love

Autumn hued mottled leaves lay strewn on the path.
Together they stroll.
Her delicate hand rests almost weightless,
Like a bit of down in his cupped hand.

From time to time he turns to study her face.
Sensing his glances, she turns her head,
Ever so slightly, lest he see the color rising in her cheeks,
Brought on by the intense emotion welling up inside her.

I Don't Want To Cry

I don't want to give in to self pity, sadness,
Wallow in those feelings.
Such weakness! Such waste!

I fight it, bake cookies, pull weeds, paint, write.

Sometimes the sad feelings go.
Other times, nothing helps, and tears flow.
That's okay, I'm only human.

Lemon Tree

Come, pick lemons
Before they fall and rot.
Wintertime, you are so prolific
When I want my tea, with milk and HOT.

Oh Lemon Tree,
Why is it when I need you most,
In summer, for my ICED tea,
You are not there for me?

January 30, 1997

Go For It

Awake! Arise! Shine!
Time slips by. Don't let it get away! Grab it!

Your hopes, your dreams, and your desires are what make you
special.
Don't get stuck in the mire of apathy, indecision, and other's
derision.

Cling to your dreams! Make them happen!
Don't abandon hope! Your life seeks fulfillment.

Blue

When we are fortunate enough to see a rainbow, its colors blending, one into another, we can only exclaim. How marvelous, this arc of beauty.

Every color is wonderful, in its own right, but if I had to pick just one as my favorite, it would have to be blue; not for color alone, but for emotions that the many shades of blue evoke.

When I think of blue, serenity comes to mind. I feel comfortable when I wear it. I can't say that it excites me, it never will, it just makes me feel good. When wearing blue, "all's right with the world".

There are so many shades of blue. Think of basic blue, the true blue. Think of the other two primary colors, red on one side, yellow on the other. Adding a bit of red to the blue or on the other side a bit of yellow to the blue, the color changes. As you add more and more red to the blue, it eventually becomes purple. Adding more and more yellow to the blue, eventually green appears. You can't possibly count all the shades in between. Add white to these shades, think of how many more values you have. Add the complimentary color, (opposite on the color wheel) you grey each of these shades and thus even more tones appear. Endless blues.

But lets get back to blue. Blues in the sky. Bodies of water that reflect the sky in its various moods. Birds, their blue feathers. Flowers: Hyacinths, a lavender blue, Iris, blue violet, Cornflowers, brilliant, happy blue, Forget Me Nots, sweet, tiny pale blue clusters, Hydrangeas, Lupines, bluebells and Texas Bluebonnets. Eyes: light blues, bright blues, dark blues, blue violets, and greenish aqua blues – BLUE.

Clothes!

Baby blue, pale blue that we associate with baby boys. How we soften, melt when we see it.

Blueberries!

Blue is all around us. Automobiles are blue, and house furnishings – from wall paint and wallpaper to carpet, upholstery, linens and china.

Sapphires!

Think of the blue of evening and night. Picture a scene of waning light. Shades of deep blue fill my head when my eyes are heavy and I'm ready for bed.

Oh BLUE, Yes BLUE ZZZZZZZZzzzzzzzzzzz

A Boiling Pot

"Give me a topic" I said to my daughter.
"I'll try writing something if I possibly can."
She glanced at her stove, a pot with boiling water.
"A boiling pot" she said.
Man oh man, that's a tough one!

Now let me see, what can I say about a boiling pot?
One thing for sure, it's got to be hot…
What will she do with it? What? What? What?

Turns out, Pot Roast is the fare for tonight.
She's cooking and waiting for it to get done.
Hours of jabbing with all her might.
The meat will not soften. No way! None.
It's a tough one!

So, what can I say re this boiling pot?
A loss and a failure, that's what she got.
Out came the franks. Finish! End! Dot.

February 1, 1997

Grandma's Arrival

I'm elated when I think that tomorrow I'll be seeing my little grandsons. It warms my heart when I picture their happy faces as I alight from the train.

Alex will be waving and shouting "Grandma, Grandma". Josh will be sitting in his stroller, somewhat bewildered, seeing the big train and grandma coming down the steps.

I arrive in L.A., and there they are, waiting on the platform, along with their Mom, my daughter. Josh's eyes, normally large, are larger now. "This is exciting", he must be thinking. As I approach him to hug and kiss him, he becomes shy and lowers his eyes. From behind, Alex throws his arms around my neck, almost choking me. I turn around and we give each other a great big loving hug.

Spending precious time with grandchildren is one of life's great pleasures. Alex is seven. Josh is two.

Grounded

Alexander learned a lesson today.
He did not listen when his father called.
He found out being disrespectful does not pay.
Now that he's grounded, he's appalled.

It's hard being a kid and having to mind,
When you'd rather be playing outside with your friends.
But a lesson must be learned of a serious kind.
When you cross certain lines, you must make amends.

Life's Cycle

INNOCENCE Tears of a babe
              like tiny dew drops
      nestled in a buttercup,
             fresh and sweet and new.

HOPE   Tears of young love
              like sparkling diamonds
      rolling down a rose petal cheek,
             endless possibilities, daydreaming,
                  anticipation.

HAPPINESS Tears of joy
              like drops of water
      dancing on a hot pot,
             marriage, children, celebrations.

REALITY   Tears of disillusion
              like icy wind-driven sleet
      cutting into the heart,
             illness, anxiety, torment.

FINALITY Tears of parting
              like drops of rain
      falling to the pavement,
             splattering, dissipating,
     separation, sadness, acceptance.

March 2, 1998

Thoughts On Differences

I often wonder, "What marriage is Peachy Dandy one hundred percent of the time?" If someone should tell me theirs is or was, I think to myself, "This is a liar, a person in denial, or an idiot who doesn't even know or won't admit when something is amiss."

Who do you know, that can agree with another person all the time? We are all different, see things differently, and come from different backgrounds. Good! If we were all the same, and saw things the same way, life would be very dull indeed.

So, two people come together, and it doesn't make sense that they will see eye to eye on all issues. The weaker person would have to give in to the stronger one and repress his or her own thoughts and desires for the sake of harmony. But, in doing so, constantly giving in, self esteem suffers. It is not healthy or wise to become a dishrag. Resentments build and the marriage suffers.

Compromise is healthy. Communication is healthy.

Arthur and Shirley

Shirley

Shirley & Phyllis

Phyllis

Morton

Arthur

Shirley

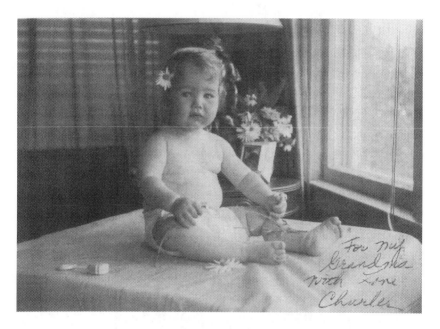

My son Charles

My daughter Anita

Anita and Dad

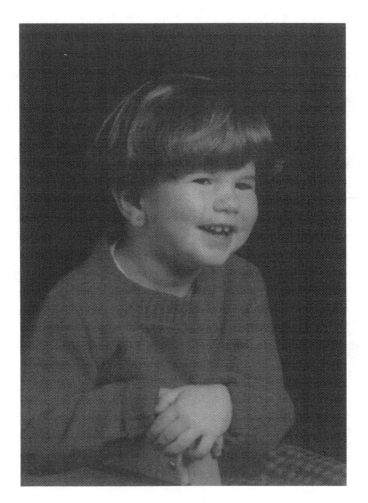

Jennifer

Joshua and Alexander

My Dad Harry

My Mother Dora

That Was Then

There was a time in my girlish days,
When I veered off in various ways.
Sampled the wine of young men's lips,
As they did mine, taking numerous sips.

Carefree, daring, a "why not" sprite,
Knowing full well, wrong from right.
Head and heart may not see eye to eye,
But I felt time was passing me by.

I had to behave as my heart dictated.
Sowed wild seeds till the need abated.
That was before I met the "One",
And then my frolicking days were done.

No, You Cannot Go Home Again

Recently, I went back to my home town, New York City, "The Big Apple". Looking at the panoramic skyline from the terrace of my friend's home, on the New Jersey side of the Hudson River directly opposite Forty-Second Street, it seemed wondrous.

Getting into the city, being immersed in it, is quite another story. I found it more crowded than I remembered, more busses than ever before, trucks, taxis, cars spewing forth toxic fumes, making breathing difficult.

Times Square, the hub, the signs larger than can be imagined. At night they come to life, garish neon, one more hideous and grotesque than the other. It made me cringe. Is bigger better?

For years I worked there, right in the heart of it all, never noticing, never bothered by any of it. I rushed to work in one of those skyscrapers in the mornings and left in the evenings to where I was going, never looking up, taking it all for granted. Living in New York, this is what you do, what everyone does. Dash, rush, push, shove...daily life in the madness that is Manhattan.

Now, I returned as a visitor, acting like any tourist in this amazing city...walking the streets, looking up at the tall buildings, my head bent back to see the tops, holding onto my purse all the while because of the many stories of muggings and snatched purses. Why do hordes of people flock here? What is it that attracts them?

I left New York State behind fifteen years ago when I moved to San Diego. For thirty-five years before then, I lived in Port Washington, a beautiful town on Long Island. It was a typical suburban lifestyle; house, garden, husband, son and daughter to raise, community activities—all of that. From time to time, I took the train into the city to do freelance art work, or to meet a friend or to shop in the big department stores. Occasionally, my husband and I drove into the city for a family function, to see a play, or attend the opera. I no longer faced the daily life of working in the city.

In the fifteen years that I have lived in San Diego, I returned to New York only half a dozen times to visit family and friends. Each time I grew more and more alienated from the life I had known back there. On this visit, I went to Port Washington, visited with friends and even rang the doorbell at my former house. Since no one answered, I walked around to the back yard, admiring my peonies and the big old cherry tree that shaded the yard.

From New Jersey, I went into the city by bus three times. I walked, taxied, looked, lunched, dined...and each time I was glad to get back to the quiet side of the river. This trip convinced me that New York was no longer my home. It's an interesting place to visit, but I could no longer live there.

July 19, 1998

How I Feel When I Am Alone And Writing

There are times when I appreciate time alone. When I have something to say that I just have to get down on paper, lest I lose the thought and it gets away from me, it is then that I am glad that nothing and no one is around to distract me.

It is hard to write, say the things you want to say, the way you want to say them, even in the quietest surroundings. But when there are voices, noises, distractions, it is almost impossible for me to concentrate.

The subject I am thinking about has a lot to do with what I write and the way I write it. If it is a subject I feel strongly about or perhaps I'm emotional about, then being alone, without distractions, I can't wait to write it. In a sense then, I am fortunate to have the time and the luxury of being able to concentrate on my writing.

Nothing comes easy. Nothing good comes without effort; nor does the end product happen by itself. It requires thought and revision, writing and rewriting until it is the best it can be. Being alone and quiet, in order to give the work the time and undivided attention it deserves, is essential to my way of thinking.

March 15, 2003

Realization

My mind says, "You can do that
And this, no sweat, a piece of cake."
Yeah, sure! I tip my hat
To those who can. I give myself a shake

And face reality. I can't move so fast,
My steps have slowed; I'm accomplishing less.
The energy I once had is in the past.
I want so much to DO…It's such a mess…

This getting old.

I'm frustrated, mad, I want to do more.
Time is running out, no way to achieve,
All that I dreamed in days before,
When I was starry-eyed and did believe,

That one day I'd be or do something great.
But, while I was dreaming, God made other plans.
He led me, directed me, sealed my fate
And placed me among the "also-rans".

August 7, 1998

Unanswered Questions

Will I ever see you again?
    Shall we meet in that place beyond,
      As we met in the heretofore
        In the park by the lily-pond?

Will I ever see you again?
    Shall you be young, in your robust state,
      As you were in those untroubled days,
        When first we began to date?

Will I ever see you again?
    Shall we once more recapture,
      As we did way back then,
        The thrill, the joy, the rapture?

Will I ever see you again?
    Shall I relive what I did before,
      As I waited for your return,
        When you came home from the war?

If ever that time should come,
    When we meet once again, on that shore,
      What will that homecoming be like?
        Will it be less, or possibly more?

Someday

An ordinary word, SOMEDAY
Consider its connotation
    Not a looking-back word
    But a looking forward word
    Uplifting with hope

Someday, we will do
Someday, we will be
Not today, not yesterday
But one day, a day yet to come

    We will grow up
    We will graduate from school
    We will be engaged in work we enjoy.
    SOMEDAY

We envision what may be ahead
We aspire to an achievement
We look ahead with anticipation
To a time in the future

    SOMEDAY

November 15, 2000

The Inevitable

Where is that little two year old,
with the pout on her face,
and the patent leather Mary Janes?

Where is the freckle-faced girl,
with knee socks, one fallen to midcalf,
and always a scrape on her knee?

What happened to the tomboy, that spirited sprite,
flying like the wind, racing,
face, inches ahead of her carrot-top curls?

Where is the teenager,
attempting to buck parental authority,
wanting to be independent and free?

"I grew up".

As I See It

In the early years of their marriage, sometime after the birth of their daughter, they came to an understanding. They loved one another, but they were no longer in love. Above all, they loved the daughter that together they had brought into this world.

He was becoming involved in politics. He was ambitious and his telescope was pointed toward Washington, D.C. He was a Rhodes Scholar, and in addition, handsome and glib, a winning combination for a man yearning for and driving along the road toward the presidency. She was a successful lawyer, in her own right.

Early on, they agreed that they would no longer share the marital bed. Their private life would be just that…Private! In public, they would present themselves as a loving couple and they did, always entering church on Sundays, holding hands; always photographed smiling, happy often with their daughter.

In their private agreement, she would do what ever it took to help him reach his goal. She was no less ambitious than he. It is common knowledge that he said, the public would be getting two for the price of one.

How she lives her private life is her business. Rumors surface from time to time, but at least she is discreet. The same cannot be said of him.

He is a ladies man and a charmer. If he has no sex life with his wife, it stands to reason that he would look for it elsewhere.

Living in the White House goldfish bowl, it is almost impossible to hide.

Time was, when former presidents had affairs, mistresses, it was kept quiet. Today, there is no such thing: Blurt it out! Get the scoop! Shock the people! Scandal! Sensationalism!

You cannot feel sorry for her. She is well aware of who she is married to. She says she is committed to this marriage, and she is, for now. What will happen after they leave the White House remains to be seen.

Pity has to be directed toward the daughter who is placed in the middle of it all, and must suffer the embarrassment. How do they answer to her?

August 30, 1998

Nothing Says Summer Like a Ripe Peach

The best peach is one you pick from the tree.
Bite into it and feel the warm juice run down your chin.
Oh the aroma! Oh the flavor!

Peaches we see in the markets
When it's winter time here,
Come from below the equator where it is summer.

In order to reach us firm and unblemished,
They are picked green and therefore are hard
And tasteless when we get them.

Give yourself a treat in season.
Get some good peaches; bake a cobbler, a pie,
Or fix peach shortcake. What could be better?

I love to make Peach Preserves.
What is so good about this is that
Summer can be extended and enjoyed all year long.

January 24, 2004

Puede Ser

¿Puede ser, que cuando nuestros ojos,
Se encontraron, tu corazon respondió como el mío?
¿Puede ser que tu me quieras
igual que yo te quiero a tí?

¿Es posible que estuvímos destinados
a estar juntos, tú y yo?
¿Es possible que Dios lo arregló que
Estuvieramos en ese lugar, en ese momento en el tiempo?

Sí puede ser, es posible, que asi sea.

Spanish Version

Can It Be

Can it be that when our eyes met
Your heart responded like mine?
Can it be that you love me
The same as I love you?

Is it possible that we were destined
To be together, you and I?
Is it possible that God arranged that
We were in that place, at that moment in time?

Yes, it can be, it is possible, it is so.

English Version

September 1, 1998

Raoul Hurd

There is a fella named Raoul
He reads with a brogue that's foul
He makes it sound real
He gives it the feel
Of an Irishman, wise as an owl.

Dick Myers

His disposition is sunny
You can be sure he'll be funny
His poems have a twist
No one can resist
His book should make plenty of money.

Nancy Webb

No one writes love stuff like she
That's simply the way it must be
Style, her very best
Passion, filled with zest
Clever gal, Lucky guy, He!

For St. Patty's Day, 2004

3 Limericks

Nunca Para Siempre

Caminando por la playa, mano en mano
Parando de vez en cuando a besar,
Estamos de pie, lado a lado, mirando al mar
Calentados por el sol y el amor que sentimos.

Deseando que este día no terminará nunca
Esperando que nuestro amor durará para siempre,
Viviendo en el momento, sin cuidado, creyendo.
Frio, triste, cuando el sueno esta muerto.

Spanish Version

Never Forever

Walking along the beach, hand in hand
Stopping from time to time, to kiss
We stand side by side, looking at the sea
Warmed by the sun and the love that we feel.

Wishing that this day will never end
Hoping that our love will last forever,
Living in the moment without care, believing.
Cold, sad, when the dream is dead.

English Version

September 2, 1998

Sometimes

Sometimes it takes but a moment
A smile, a wink, a glance.
You don't need more than that moment
To fall in love, by chance.

Sometimes love grows slowly.
It may not start off with a spark,
But its flames grow bigger and brighter,
Long after others turned dark.

July 19 1998

Before It's Too Late

This week in a telephone conversation with my daughter, I told her: "The best thing I ever did in my life, was to adopt you". She said: "Thank you Mom, it was so sweet of you to tell me that and the best thing in my life is having you for my mother."

I will not be able to say this to my child, nor will she be able to say what she did, after I am gone. It is so very important to express your love, your feelings while you are able and not hold back until it is too late.

I was forty-five years old, my husband forty-eight, when we received word that a baby girl was available for adoption. We were told that we had three days to make up our minds.

Our son, adopted five years before was everything in the world to us, besides, he was picture perfect. How could there ever be another child who would measure up? We discussed it, we agonized, we wavered, we could not decide. I made a list, "For and Against".

On the For side, there were only three things:

1. We would have a daughter.
2. My son would not be a lonely only child.
3. He kept asking for a sister.

On the Against side, there was a long list:

1. We were too old to adopt another child.
2. Our son would be starting school in the fall, and now we would have to start all over again with an infant.
3. What about the expense involved in raising another child? And on and on…

When it came time to give our answer, I made the call still unsure. I blurted out, "We'll take her". My heart overruled my head. We never even for one minute regretted it. God graced us with a beauty, a girl with many talents, but above all, a beautiful character.

Now, she is grown, married and with two little boys of her own. I am getting along in years, and I realize how important it is not to put off things that need to be said.

DO IT NOW!!

September 4, 1998

Mamala

"Mamala" they called me,
My daddy and his brothers,
Six of them in all.

Why did they call me Mamala?
What does this word mean?

Named for their mother,
Their mama, who died so young of asthma.
She was only forty-two.

Adding "la" on to Mama,
Makes it diminutive.

"Little Mama" told me they loved me,
As they loved their mother who had left them,
Through no fault of her own.

Until the day my dad left me, to join her in heaven,
I remained his "Mamala".

Red Carnations

Carnations, my favorite flowers!
I have always loved their spicy fragrance,
Long stems and narrow graceful leaves.

I look at them and study their beauty.
Many petals cluster in the flower head,
Each one zigzag edged, as if cut with pinking shears.
They come in a wide variety of colors.
Some are streaked, red on white, like peppermint candies.

Carnations have a special meaning for me.
Knowing how I love them,
"He" always had the florist slip some
Into a bouquet on my birthday or our anniversary.
On Valentine's Day every year
"He" brought me a bouquet of only RED CARNATIONS.

February 5, 1999

Alone

I hate being alone.
I hate it with a passion.
There is no one to talk to,
When I sit here in this fashion.

Alone, is a lonely state.
Feelings are buried deep.
To whom can you let them out?
All you want to do, is sleep.

Sleep is an opiate,
But, then when you awaken,
There you are again,
Alone and sadly shaken.

Grandpa

Grandpa was a handsome gent. We kids loved seeing him approach, as he walked along DeKalb Avenue, coming from the Franklin Avenue trolley stop to the corner of Emerson Place where our grocery store was situated.

I never saw Grandpa in anything but a three piece grey suit, with his watch chain strung across the vest. On his head he wore a Panama straw hat. He had a square face and a gray Vandyke beard, neatly trimmed.

He was in the real estate business and his whole demeanor at all times looked as if he could at any moment be about to close a big Real Estate Deal. Grandpa was a distinguished man yet, should a pretty girl walk by, Grandpa winked. When questioned about this practice, he said, "The Eye needs something".

September 21, 2000

Coincidence

Someone recently talked about magic or what we may call coincidence. For instance, thinking of someone and a letter from that person arrives or the phone rings. I pick up, say "Hello Anita" (my daughter). She asks, "How did you know it was me?" I reply, "I was just thinking of you, so I knew it had to be you". "Mom, I always said you were a witch".

From time to time, I send some of my poems to a cousin who lives in the state of Washington. A while back she wrote, "My nephew's uncle is Robert Hass the Poet Laureate". She mentioned that his new book is called "Sun Under Wood". I jotted it on a piece of paper…Sun Under Wood – Robert Hass, intending when I got to Barnes and Noble, to check it out.

Sometime later, going through papers on the kitchen counter, I came across that slip of paper just before running out to pick up milk. My car radio is always set on PBS and when I turned on the ignition, I heard a man reading a poem about a mother speaking of her newborn child. A touching poem, I was impressed with the reading of it as well as the content. I parked my car in the market parking lot and continued to listen. The reader was Robert Hass, former Poet Laureate of the United States. He had compiled a book of poems by other writers called "Poets Choice/Poems for Everyday Life" and he was reading from it. I sat in my car for twenty minutes, until the station break, listening in awe and wonder.

I thought "What a coincidence that just this afternoon I came across the piece of paper with his name on it and here he is on the radio reading a beautiful poem to me". When I arrived home, I dashed off a note to my cousin telling her how pleased I was to meet Robert Hass, even though it wasn't in person.

Magic, coincidence, what would you call it? If I had read the poems myself, that would have been good, but to have a poet laureate read them to me, was a special privilege.

November 11, 1999

My Prayer For The New Year

On Rosh Hashanah, the beginning of the New Year
I will start off on a blank page.
I will start off unblemished, unsullied,
Like a baby, just born.

I can not nor do I want to ask of G-d
To keep the pages of my book clean and empty,
For that will mean that I have done nothing,
That I have not lived.

Rather, let my pages be filled full, even the margins
From the beginning of the book of Tishrei, 5764
To the end of Elul. Full of worthwhile things I have done
Full of words I have uttered, that matter and make sense.

Let me be the Shofar that calls forth my loved ones
To be good and to do good, for the betterment of man.
Let me be the clay in G-d's hands
That he will mold into a better human being.

What I do ask of G-d in all my prayers, in all humility,
That he sees fit to keep me and my loved ones safe from harm
And that He sees to it, to help people all over the world,
To live in harmony and to learn love instead of hate.

Please G-d, let there never again be war, only PEACE!
And on Yom Kippur, may it be sealed.

September 14, 2003

Is It Ever Too Late?

Is it ever too late?
Too late for what?
What is it you want?
                    Companionship!

Someone to talk with, or listen to
Or not have to talk with at all.
Just sit with, be with, walk with
Play a game of scrabble with.

Prepare a meal together, eat together
It's no fun to cook for one's self
Then eat alone, on a T.V. table.

Someone to drive beside,
Go to the park with, or the beach
Maybe stop for coffee along the way
People watch and laugh about.

Visit the Rose Garden in the park
Admire the variety, the beauty
Photograph the flowers and each other.

Eat a bon-bon; pass the box along to someone else.
Watch T.V., comment to someone, not the empty room.
Admire, compliment another or be complimented by them.

Bring someone flowers, a book, a trinket.
The value is in the giving
And the pleasure it gives to another.
Not the amount spent.

Greet someone with a hug or kiss.
Go to a movie, play or concert,
And hold hands.

Smile!
When alone, who are you going to smile at?
Yourself in the mirror?
Read aloud, something that you want to share.

Far away friends, who you correspond with,
Talk with on the phone, are wonderful,
But not as warm as a friend beside you.

Many of these pastimes can be done alone,
And often you want to do them alone, be alone.
But, isn't it nice, when you want to share with another
That there is someone to share them with?

Lucky is the person, who can find
That special someone we want to be with,
And who wants to be companions with us.

"No, it is never too late."

Green

Green, like Jade is green
Like the paler underside of a leaf, that green
Like the dark that can be seen
When gazing deep into a whirlpool
Spiraling shades of green, those greens
Leaves, carried along
On a swiftly moving giggling brook
Dancing over moss covered stones, these greens
Eyes, like limpid pools, this green
Green as our youth,
When all the world was Green.

April 27, 1999

Diddley Squat and Tiddley Winks

Diddley Squat and Tiddley Winks
Were walking, holding hands.
"Isn't this a marvelous place?" he asked.
"Yes", she replied, "a wonderland".

The moss was soft beneath their feet.
From the canopy of trees and leaves,
Bits of sunshine filtered through,
Like attic windows under eaves.
   That was the day they walked in the woods.

Diddley Squat and Tiddley Winks
While walking hand in hand,
Made a dash to the waters edge,
Their feet were burning from the hot, hot sand.

"Ow! Wow! This hurts," howled Diddley,
"I should have worn my shoes".
"And I hate sand between my toes".
Whined Tiddley, mid "Yoiks" and "Eeks" and "Oohs".
   That was the day they went to the beach.

"Next time we're out and it's humid and hot,
Let's go back", said Tiddley, "to the nice cool woods,
Where it's shady and quiet and we can hold hands,
Or sit on a log eating picnic foods".

"The beach is no place on such a hot day
With the sun beating down so we have to flee.
We'll go back as you say to the cool, cool woods.
Yes Tiddley, you're right", said Diddley, "I have to agree".
    And that is exactly what they did.

My Collection

In the spring before we married, Jerry took me to Toronto, to meet his family for the first time. One day, while there, we went to Chinatown. We stopped into a gift shop. I fell in love with a pair of blue and white porcelain jars. Jerry bought them for me. Little did I know on that day that those two pieces would be just the beginning of a fifty year accumulation, my collection of blue and white china.

Members of my family gave me a piece for my birthday or anniversary, or brought back a piece as a gift, when they traveled to a foreign country. Originally I kept the blue and white confined to my bedroom and the kitchen. As years went by, and the collection grew, it spilled over into other rooms in the house. In my own travels, I was always drawn to the blue and white and couldn't resist something attractive when I happened upon it.

I felt that one day it would go to my daughter, especially when I saw her lean toward the blue in her rented house. This past year, I saw her taste change. When she moved into the big new house, she furnished it in earth tones, and kept the blue and white in only the guest room which I occupy when I visit her.

I wonder, what will become of my collection, after I am gone? When you start a collection, you do it for yourself. Something about the items appeals to you, to make you want to keep it and add to it. Watching it grow and expand over the years, aside from the fact that it has value, you plan in your own mind that eventually it will go to your daughter. Who better than she understands how much your collection means to you, and you assume for that reason alone, it will mean a lot to her.

This is a wrong assumption to make. She is a grown woman and has her own taste and preferences. Still, it is a big disappointment to me. I hate the thought that what took years to accumulate, may be dissipated, sold off or given away to strangers.

Not too long ago, when I visited one of my sisters-in-law who had some blue and white china, she gave me several pieces, and sent with me a few for Anita. Her reason being that she felt her daughter-in-law would not want it, and she made up her mind to give it to those she knew who would appreciate it. This could be one of my options. Another might be to sell it myself. I really don't want to do either. When I mentioned my concerns to Anita, she said she would never get rid of it.

Storing it in her garage, eventually it will be broken. Her husband periodically cleans out the garage, I can see it being sold for peanuts at one of their garage sales. Why should I feel sad about this? But I do. Not just the collection is in danger, but my whole household. What it took a lifetime to build may come to nothing.

There is always hope that Anita's taste may change. Mine did. After my father died, we moved to a new apartment. My brother, twenty and I, eighteen, wanted new things, modern. Mom said, "Go ahead, do what you want". We put many things away in the cellar, things we felt were old fashioned. After a while we tired of the modern stuff and little by little began to bring pieces back upstairs. Some of it I have in my home today. Anita, "if" she holds on to my treasures, may one day do the same.

A Dream

While away the hours
    While away the day
        Dreaming dreams
            Thinking thoughts.

Is time being wasted
    Or are seeds being planted
        So, that later,
            Ideas may be harvested?

Dreamers have dreamt
    Thinkers have thought
        Incredible accomplishments
            Started with a dream.

July 1997

Cheese

Munching on a slice of Muenster
Prompted me to be a funster.
Pad before me, pen in my hand
How will this take off? Where will it land?

Feta in salad, Brie with fresh pear
Parmesan on pasta, excellent fare.
Swiss cheese sandwiches, mustard and pickle
Oh, my palate is starting to tickle.

Ricotta, Mozzarella in lasagna, tutto bella.
Camembert, Monrachet and Chavrie, oui, oui,
No matter what country, no matter where
You'll find some kind of cheese most everywhere.

My personal favorite, versatile cream
Baked in a cheese cake, short of a dream
Or pie; or tarts, a delicious delight
Welcomed anytime, morn, noon or night.

Cream cheese and olives, cream cheese with jelly
Or spread on a bagel with lox from the deli.
From tulipland come Edam and Gouda. Eat'em! Good-a!
Danish Havarti or Swiss Gruyere, I don't care, I love'em all.

Gorgonzola, Roquefort, Stilton and Blue
Marble-veined beauties, wonderful too.
Goat cheese on toast, melted Jack or Cheddar
What if anything could be better
        than CHEESE?

1997

Violin

The violin has heart, the violin has soul, when played by someone with like qualities who fingers the strings and slides the bow across them with feeling, sensitivity and understanding of the music.

Stradivarius and Amati are the gems of violins. It is the dream of serious violinists to own one, but only a few are so privileged and so blessed.

My brother had a fine fiddle, not a Strad or Amati by any means but as good an instrument as my parents could afford, at that time. It was made in Italy, in 1928, not far from being an antique, now. Arthur played very well.

When my daughter showed an interest we bought her a half size violin. When you grow into a full size violin, I will give you this one, her uncle promised. After he passed away, Aunt Doris, remembering that promise, gave Anita his violin. She played it lovingly and proudly in the orchestras in elementary, junior high and even held first chair in her high school orchestra.

After high school, Anita went to Israel on a work study program for one year. She couldn't conceive of being separated from her violin for all that time, so she removed some of her clothes from her trunk, in order to make room for her instrument. Her violin traveled from New York to Israel, accompanied her on her travels in Europe and back to New York. Later when our family relocated to San Diego the violin moved with us, and again from San Diego to Los Angeles.

The violin was set aside, while Anita completed her college education, became a teacher, married and began the process of raising her two sons, Alexander now ten, and Joshua five.

Alex plays Alto Sax in his school orchestra. When recently as a family we attended the Spring Concert, Joshua said, "I love the sound of the violins and I would like to take lessons". That struck a chord in me. I questioned Anita about her violin. She told me that the bridge needs repair and the bow needs to be re-haired. I asked her to please take it to be restored, I would pay for it, and this will be my birthday present to her. My thinking is that maybe she will be inclined to pick it up and play on occasion and perhaps one day she will pass it along to Joshua.

We went together to Thomas Metzler, violin maker in Pasadena and had her violin put into good working order. Next, we went to Old Town Music Co. and rented a 1/8 size violin for Joshua. I paid for the first month's rent. He is taking lessons from Louise Brown, and enjoys it. It gives me a great deal of pleasure when I see Anita playing along with Joshua.

The violin is the soprano of the orchestra. It carries the melody. There are moments when a violin solo brings tears to my eyes. Piano, Cello, Flute and Harp are beautiful instruments, and wonderful music has been written for them, but none of these can tear at my heartstrings like the melodic tones that come from the Violin.

June 16, 2002

Saturday's Dilemma

Shall I take out my paints and paint?
Shall I go make up my bed?
Shall I water the indoor plants?
Or clean the house instead?

Shall I answer some letters I owe?
Shall I get to the bank before two?
Shall I sit down and write for class?
Yes, that is what I will do.

May 17, 1997

Life Is Fleeting

When we are young, we think of
our lifetime ahead as Eternity.
As our days draw to a close,
We come to realize that in the
scheme of things, our life on this planet
is nothing but a puff of air, here
but for a moment and blown away,
like a dandelion that has gone to seed,
that you pluck and blow and watch
the fluff scatter and fly away.

April 1997

Give It Time

Heartaches strike unannounced
Shock us with suddenness
Cut down lives in their prime
Rob us of companionship unfulfilled.
      Give it time, they say.

Can time fill a hole?
Can time sew a torn heart?
Can time dry tears
When they flow uncontrolled?
Can time make the emptiness go away?
      Give it time, they say.

What pain for parents to lose a child.
No grandchildren to carry on.
Dreams and plans shot to pieces
In the depth of despair
What can one say, except…
      Give it time!

The Monarchy and the Betrayal of Diana

Crash! The Mercedes struck a pillar. Princess Diana's life came to an abrupt end. Laid to rest three days ago, the sadness lingers. Young, beautiful, two fine sons, a new love affair, just when her life seemed to be taking an upturn, she was cut down.

A search for a suitable bride for Charles, Prince of Wales, and heir to the throne of England took place. She had to come from the nobility. This was a priority, for one day she would be queen.

Diana was chosen. Nineteen years old when she and the prince married. She was only four years older than her son, Prince William, is today. It was a fairy tale wedding, covered by the media and watched on television by five and one-half billion worldwide. In due time, Prince William arrived, followed three years later by Prince Harry.

Soon after, it came to light that Charles had been seeing his former lady-love, Camilla Parker Bowles, right along. Diana was betrayed. Charles married her just so she would produce an heir to the throne. What a terrible thing to do to her. How must she have felt? What about her self-esteem when she realized why he married her. He admitted in an interview that he never loved her at all.

Geraldine Ferraro, on the "Crossfire" program referred to Prince William as the heir, and Prince Harry as the backup. Diana gave Charles what he wanted from her and then he needed her no more. How that low character could deceive his young wife, use her and cause her such pain and embarrassment is unforgivable. How will he explain all this to his sons in time to come? As for the queen, I feel she knew full well that Charles loved Camilla. How could she permit him to do this to Diana, for the sake of succession. She is as guilty as he.

If this is what the monarchy stands for, if such despicable injustice is condoned, then it is time England gives serious thought to change. British pomp and pageantry is colorful and good for tourism. People love to visit castles and palaces. Kings, queens, princes and princesses are storybook characters out of times past and should be relegated to museums. In my opinion, it is a tradition whose purpose has passed. It does not belong in the twenty-first century.

September 9, 1997

Gloria, Mi Amiga, My Friend

She came from Puerto Rico to Brooklyn, New York along with her mother, two brothers, Acisclo and Manuel and two younger sisters, Luz Lavinia (Lucy) and Maria Rafaela (Pepela). Gloria was ten years old, so was I. We became friends and have remained friends to this day.

Earlier on, Juan (John), Jaime (James) Rosendo, and sisters: Rosa Maria (Rose) and Carmen came to Brooklyn. They got jobs, rented an apartment, and set up a household for when their mother and the five youngest children would arrive.

One day, Mrs. Bou came into our grocery store with one of the older children who could translate, to ask for credit until one of the siblings got his paycheck. My mother obliged. Mrs. Bou was a widow, raising a big family. She and my mom struck up a friendship of a kind. She spoke no English, my mother spoke no Spanish, but always one of the children came with her to interpret. The younger children were enrolled in P.S. 45. This was the elementary school which I attended and it was directly across the street from our store. Before long they knew enough English to come and shop or to come with their mother. Mrs. Bou and my mom had many a fine conversation and visit with the help of the interpreters. For years, my mother extended credit to the Bou family as they needed it. When they were paid they sometimes paid their bill in full, but more often than not, there was a balance which added up over the years. When Acisclo was old enough and began to work, he took it upon himself to come to my mother each week when he was paid and give her some money toward paying off the bill. Eventually he alone paid every last cent. My mother thought so much of him because of this. My mother never closed the store, even to attend family functions. She felt she had to keep her store open to accommodate customers who depended on her to feed their families. They bought on credit and paid her as they could, sometimes not at all. My mom felt that God helped her provide for her family and if she could help others at the same time, she felt good about that. There was a time when Acisclo took sick. He had a collapsed lung. Then and only then, did Mama close the store and go to visit him in the hospital. She never forgot his goodness and how he took on the responsibility of paying back the family debt. She held him in the highest regard. Acisclo recovered and he went back to work. His boss had a retail clothing store. When he grew old and felt it was time to retire he offered the business to Acisclo. Acisclo bought the business and was very successful. He was a person of good moral character. He married, raised a family and lived a good long life. He died in August, 2003 at eighty seven years of age, and I mourn his passing.

Gloria was born on Sabado de Gloria, the Saturday before Easter, and that is why she was given the name Gloria. She spent many hours with me in the kitchen in back of our store. I spent many hours with her and her family in their apartment. In our teens on Saturdays we often went into Manhattan. Gloria took me to Mass at St. Patrick's Cathedral. I took her to services at Temple Emanuel. We visited The Metropolitan Museum of Art and The Museum of Natural History together. We were discovering and learning to broaden our horizons together. Gloria is Catholic. I am Jewish. We learned about each other's religions. When Gloria made a Novena, I asked questions. When she went to confession I went with her and waited outside. As soon as she came out, I started to question her "What do you do in there?" I remember still, "Bless me Father, for I have sinned, it is one month since my last confession…" And then she was given her penance "Say ten Hail Mary's, and five Our Fathers." I never forgot what I learned from her at that time, and she still remembers many of the things she learned from me and my family about our religion.

Before Christmas, I helped Gloria dress the tree. Since they were a large family no one could give all the others a gift, so, all the names were placed in a bowl and each person picked one, and that was the only person you had to buy a gift for. The only persons who received more were Mama and Pepela, the youngest. Mama cooked the familiar favorites which everyone enjoyed, including me. I remember Pasteles, Arroz Con Pollo, Platanos, Flan and Arroz Con Dulce. After eating, the rug was rolled up, furniture moved, phonograph turned on and dancing commenced. It was a happy time in that home. In our home there was no such merriment. Our store was open to serve the customers, so I looked for every opportunity to go to Gloria's house where there were lots of people and fun and laughter.

When Gloria's younger brother Manuel was about ten years old, he went with some boys to a swimming pool on a hot summer day. When they got there, they found it was ladies' day and they couldn't get in. So off they went to Gowanus Canal where there was no lifeguard. They jumped into the water. Manuel couldn't swim and he went under. His friends tried to find him, but he was gone. That was a sad time. Mrs. Bou said, "I lost two husbands, but that was not as bad as losing one child."

It was Christmas vacation of my first year at The Traphagen School of Fashion. I had planned to go to a formal dance on New Years Eve. I brought home two gowns and tried them on for Daddy's approval. He said, "They look so beautiful on you, keep them both." I remember them still. Daddy never did get to see me go out in one of the gowns on New Years Eve, because he died on December 27th, just a few days before. Gloria tells how I pulled her into the car as I was getting in on the day of the funeral. I wanted her to be with me at the cemetery. Gloria, like Asisclo has a good heart. She is a kind person, and I could always count on her.

Looking back, I recall how my graduation day was drawing close and my dress was still not finished. It was Gloria, who came to my aid and helped me finish the dress on time.

When we were still quite young, Gloria would tell me about Puerto Rico. She loved to run around barefoot. Quite often she would stub her toe and she would let out a stream of curses, "Mierda, cuño, carajo." I only remember the meaning of the first one, and a good thing too, because they were ugly as I recall.

Quite often, Gloria would say, "Someday I'll take you to Puerto Rico". Gloria had been taking a drug to which she had a very bad reaction. One day, on T.V. she saw something about a class action suit having to do with that particular drug. There was a phone number to call. She did, and became part of the suit. It took a long time for the case to be settled. Many times she would tell me, "Don't forget, when the case is settled, we are going to Puerto Rico." The day came when she received the settlement and she called to tell me. "Get ready, we are going." She kept her word, her promise, made so long ago. I had a wonderful time touring the island and I especially enjoyed the town of Ponce with its art museum and its beautiful architecture. While we were there Gloria's sister, Maya, celebrated her 90th birthday and members of the family came from far away to celebrate. I was happy to share in the festivities and to see once again many members of the family whom I hadn't seen in a very long time.

Gloria is my friend of longest standing. She lives on the East Coast, I on the West Coast, but we talk on the phone for long periods of time. It is amazing how much we are able to recall about our youth and the many activities we shared, way back when.

February 9, 2004

Ageless Dilemma

How will I tell my folks?
You know they'll be shocked, for sure.
No parents want to see their child go.
Can't you see what they'll have to endure?

They'll be fearful and worried, you know.
I too will be lonesome and blue.
Parting for parents and child
Is heartbreaking, tender and true.

What kind of life will we lead?
How can I leave those I love?
Where will we settle, oh where?
Lord guide us please, from above.

Parents want their child to be happy.
They need assurance. What else can they do?
Parents are protective. I too am afraid,
Even though, I truly love you.

This is a universal dilemma, since the beginning of time.
Still no one would break away, leave home
If they didn't overcome this fear
And move on, to start a unit of their own.

October 4, 2003

To Write Or Not To Write

In order to write, I need to be inspired. Sometimes, thoughts and ideas, like bananas come in bunches. Other times, zilch, nada! Then I think: "What am I doing here? Who am I kidding? I don't have anything to say."

I am reminded of an incident that took place many years ago, when I was nineteen. In the fall, I returned to the Traphagen School of Fashion for the second year of the course I was enrolled in. Jan, one of my classmates asked what I did during the summer. Her parents had taken her to Europe. I told her I went downtown. In other words, I had not done anything terribly exciting. Sarcastically, she said, "Why don't you write a book?" I felt bad. What a snob!

That evening, I told my brother about the incident. He said, "You could probably write a better book about your summer than she could write about hers."

September 11, 1997

Happy Endings

It doesn't matter
    what you experience
        in your lifetime…

The ups, the downs,
    good times, bad times,
        joys, heartaches,
        surprises, disappointments

Which one of us
    doesn't have a story
        to tell?

What does matter is,
    having survived the negatives
        surely the positives in life
            must have outweighed the other.

Friends, let's celebrate the happy endings.

    We're here!

The Indefinable "IT"

Ever find yourself surrounded
By people and still feel alone?

Ever look in closets filled with clothes
And feel there is nothing to wear?

Ever have a refrigerator full of food
And still find nothing to eat?

Abundance everywhere and yet,
We search for "IT", be it person,
Or thing that will fulfill our longings
And make our hearts sing.

September 16, 1997

An Inscription for Joshua

Dear Joshua,

As I write this letter, you have just reached your first milestone, your first birthday. Although a baby today, I trust that you will keep this book, treasure it and read it from time to time.

I have written it as one adult to another; so that in time to come, you will know your grandma Shirley a bit better, understand who she is, what she stands for, and what she accomplished in her life.

I am sorry that you and your Grandpa Jerry never had a chance to meet and know one another. He passed away five days before you were born, but you carry on his name, and that way you will always be close to him and reminded of him. I know he would have loved you, because you are someone special.

I hope you will have a wonderful life, meaningful and productive. No matter where the road leads you, always know that I love you.

October 1997

I made up a book for Joshua, just as I did for Alexander.

Snowman

Funny, funny snowman,
Round and worry-free,
Except that he is grounded,
Not like you and me.

His smile so sweet and jolly
Curved up with cranberries red.
Bedecked with a carrot nose
And top hat square on his head.

Why does he hold a broom?
What is he going to sweep?
See the plaid scarf around his neck?
I gave it to him to keep.

How will it keep him warm,
When he's made up of cold wet snow?
Standing outside all alone,
There's nowhere he can go.

If we bring him inside, he'll melt.
That's not the right thing to do.
Let him remain where he is,
And bring joy to me and you.

December 14, 2000

The Radetsky March – New Years Concert

Time: January 1, 1998
Setting: The Splendid Vienna Verein Hall
Occasion: The annual New Years Concert
Narrator: Walter Cronkite
Players: The Vienna Philharmonic Orchestra
Conductor: Zubin Mehta

It is the last encore. Walter Cronkite says, "And now, The Radetsky March, I cannot imagine this concert ending any other way."

Zubin Mehta lifts his hands, the music begins and abruptly stops. Mehta turns around to face the audience and smiles roguishly. The audience smiles back, waits. They know that this is when the conductor greets them. Mehta says, "Meine Dammen und Herren (Ladies and Gentlemen): For the first time my country, India, is watching." Pause... Then in German, he says, "I wish you all Happy New Year, from the bottom of my heart". The whole orchestra as one voice calls out, "Freuliche Neiyahr" (Happy New Year). Starting the music, stopping, addressing the people, this little game they have come to expect and await eagerly. The march resumes...Dah dah dum, dah dah dum, dah dah dum, dah dum the audience responds.

I watch the performance from my chair, at home in San Diego, joining those attending the concert in that magnificent hall in Vienna, along with watchers and listeners all over the world. We put our palms together and clap in unison, in time to the music. Dah dah dum, dah dah dum, dah dah dum, dah dum. What a beautiful tradition, joining hands in music!

January 1,1998

Loehmann's

Looking through one of my bookcases recently, I came across a book by Erma Bombeck titled "All I Know About Animal Behavior, I Learned In Loehmann's Dressing Room". I must have bought the book because it was on sale and besides, I enjoy Erma Bombeck's humor, but I never got around to reading it. I took it from the shelf and put it on the table beside my favorite chair. I intend to read it soon.

Oh the memories that title conjured up. My best friend Debby and I went many times to the original Loehmann's on Bedford Ave. in Brooklyn, looking for that perfect dress, or if we couldn't find it, well, at least a bargain of some kind. Going to Loehmann's was an adventure.

Mrs. Loehmann went to the better fashion manufacturers and bought up job lots and samples. The special garments were kept in a separate room on the second floor. If you were fortunate enough to find something you liked that fit you, you got an unbelievable bargain. On the main floor were racks of clothes on hangers, unusual things, and there were huge tables, piled high with perhaps silk blouses, or Cashmere sweaters at very low prices. Everyone loves a bargain, and this was the place to go to get something out of the ordinary at a price.

The corner store was very large, the main part of it open to the ceiling of the second floor. Show windows faced both streets, and in them there were weird manikins dressed in some mighty strange outfits, and some of these were spotted around inside the store as well.

There was a huge ornate iron, circular staircase leading to the upper floor. Midway, on a landing, like a hawk, stood Mrs. Loehmann herself, looking down on the main floor, watching that no one shoplifted. She was like a fixture, as strange as her manikins, always there, whenever we came into the store. If ever she unglued herself from that spot, it must have been after hours.

Also on the main floor was the communal dressing room. I found it embarrassing to go in there and get undressed to try on clothes. I was used to doing this in a private dressing room. At Loehmann's there was no such thing as privacy. People got undressed, many brazenly so, with nothing on except perhaps panties. You looked around and saw every kind of shape, some heavyset, attempting to squeeze into a petite size. What was most annoying was the person standing by you, waiting for you to take the garment off, so they could pounce on it to try it on. Loehmann's is definitely not Nieman Marcus.

At this point in writing, I went for the book to see what Erma had to say on the subject. After thumbing through, I came across her comments and I quote verbatim, *"For a bargain we suffer the humiliation of communal dressing rooms, surrounded by women wearing only knee highs and a handbag. Shopping has become more aggressive and violent. The women in white gloves who regarded browsing in the department stores as a pleasant outing, turned into Pit Bulls with attitudes."*

Still, Mrs. Loehmann developed a following, grew in New York City and opened more stores. I was pleasantly surprised to find Loehmann stores in California. when I moved to the West Coast. I went to one in San Diego, and although the lady and the staircase were missing, the communal dressing room with the varied shaped Pit Bulls prevailed. The Loehmann's legacy remains even now, so many years later.

Tompkins Cove

Country lanes, split rail fences
Remembering, awakens the senses
Oaks and Maples, stately and tall
Bare branches waiting for snow to fall.

We came for the weekend, New Years Eve.
To Tompkins Cove, where we'd been before
Many times in summer, autumn too,
For the changing leaves, good food and more.

We loved returning to this magical place
Where we enjoyed fresh air and open space.
Far from the city, away from the din
To this familiar retreat that we found pleasure in.

We came in a group as we always did,
Brothers, sisters and various friends
Girls bunked together, boys did the same
Unlike today's very different trends.

Not that we slept very much at all,
For after the party in the main lodge
We'd gather together in one of the rooms,
Tell jokes and stories, a real hodgepodge.
But fun we had back then, by Jove!
In our youthful days at Tompkins Cove.

January 8, 1998

237

My Reflection

At times:
> I see my reflection in the mirror.
>> I see a woman, good figure,
>>> Attractive and I think,
>>>> "Mmm, not too bad for an old girl."

Other times:
> I look in the mirror
>> And see my mother
>>> Looking back at me.
>>>> It's a bit of a shock.

Sometimes:
> When I look in the mirror,
>> Upon awakening,
>>> Hair disheveled, no makeup,
>>>> Eyes half closed…

These times:
> I look horrible enough,
>> That I scare myself.
>>> I hop into the shower,
>>>> Brush my teeth and hair,

Drag myself into the kitchen,
Have my morning tea,
Come alive
And begin to feel,
And look like my true self.

May 8, 2004

Feliz Ano Nuevo

Cuba is very much in the news this week because the Pope is visiting there. We see him on T.V. and we see Fidel Castro as well.

This brought to mind something that took place many years ago. Fidel Castro was in the United States. My mother read in the newspaper that he was so paranoid, so distrustful, that he cooked his own food in his hotel room. This prompted her to write to him. She wrote, "Instead of sitting in your hotel room and cooking your own food, why don't you get out, look around and see what a wonderful country this is." The thing is that she wrote it on the back of a New Year's card which someone had sent to her.

Lo and behold, one day a letter arrived from Cuba from the office of the prime Minister. No mention of my mother's comments and criticism…only thanks for the New Year wishes, which was not what she had intended at all.

I knew I had this letter once, so I went to my storage closet today, pulled out the carton marked "Memories", sat down on the floor in the hall and proceeded to go through it, stopping as I went along to read one thing or another that grabbed my attention. Practically at the bottom of the box I found what I was looking for. Inside the yellowed envelope was this letter, complete with official crest and numbered stamp, dated October 11, 1960:

Dear Mrs. Greenberg:

Your very nice card conveying best wishes for a Happy New Year to Dr. Fidel Castro has been very much appreciated.

We wish to assure you that our Leader is struggling not only for the independence and sovereignty of our country but also for the oppressed peoples all over the world. Equality of rights will bring about Peace and Happiness to everyone.

I assure you of my personal appreciation, and remain,

Yours very truly,

Dr. Juan A Ortega
Executive Director

The story of my mother writing to the head of a foreign country, and on the back of a greeting card which she had received no less, has long been a joke within our family. Mama never did see the humor in it.

January 24, 1998

I Got My Wish

It is September of 1930. Mom and Dad make their semi-annual trip to the wholesale house to buy our clothes for Fall and Winter. They come home, put our things away in our rooms. We have a storeroom. Daddy packs boxes on the shelves. After a while, Arthur (two years older than me) and I being curious, go into the storeroom to see what those boxes contain. We read aloud: DI-A-PERS, and again, DI-A-PERS- Diapers!!

We look at one another, mouths agape. An electric light bulb looms over our heads. "I bet Mama is going to have a baby!"

Arthur bribes Morty, our younger brother. "I'll give you a nickel, say you want a brother." I feel it is unfair they each have a brother. I offer Morty a dime. "Say you want a sister." I want a sister so badly.

I am wakened early, dressed and rushed out of the house, along with my brothers. A strange woman is in the house. We go around the corner to our grocery store to have our breakfast as we do every morning. Daddy makes cocoa. Arthur and I spread cream cheese on Uneeda Biscuits, our usual breakfast.

Daddy says: When you come home for lunch, don't go to the house, come back to the store. We do. Why does Daddy say this? What is going on? I am suspicious. Could Mama be having the baby?

At three o'clock, when I get out of school, I will go directly to the house. I am very excited: Maybe Mama has the baby. Maybe I am doing a bad thing going to the house, but, Daddy didn't say, "Come to the store after school."

We live on the top floor, four flights up. My heart is beating so fast. I hurry up the first flight and meet my brothers coming down. They too are excited as they shout: "We have a sister." That's all I hear as I fly up the remaining three flights and race into my mother's bedroom. She is in bed and my beautiful baby sister is bundled up beside her. I can't believe what I see. "God must have heard me," I say to myself.

"What will her name be?" I ask. She is to be named for my mother's mother. First initial P, second L the nurse says, "How about' Pauline?" "Oh No," I say, "No sister of mine will be named Pauline. Her name will be Phyllis." Mama and Daddy agree and give her the name Leah, for her middle name.

This is the day my sister, Phyllis Leah, is born, November 13, 1930.

Today

Yesterday, gone
Tomorrow, unknown
Do it now
Don't put it off
Today...Only Today

You may look back
To a coming yesterday
Think, "I should have"
"It might have been"
Today...Only Today

Tomorrow is a maybe
Tomorrow may never be
Don't have regrets
Do it now! Live now!
Today...Only Today

November 20, 2003

244

Old Girls

We're powdered, painted, hair done up in curls.
We're still here to talk about things.
This is where it's at.
Hooray for us...Old Girls!

It's not where it always was.
Not what we used to be.
This is what we are today.
And hooray for us...Old Girls!

We can laugh about it.
We can tell about it.
There's life in us still.
Hooray for us...Old Girls!

November 22, 2003

In My Memory

IN MY MEMORY:
> I see love sparkling in your eyes.
> It lifts my spirit to the skies.
> I see the smile upon your face,
> And, I am locked in your embrace.

IN MY MEMORY:
> Times I sensed desire in your touch.
> I loved you then so very much.
> But, memories alone do not suffice,
> Though, while it lasted it was nice.

IN MY MEMORY:
> I see us young with zest for life,
> And recall the day I became your wife.
> Who knew then, what fate had in store?
> Fifty years together is a pretty good score.

IN MY MEMORY:
> Up-sides and down-sides, good times and bad,
> Times we shared laughter, times we were mad.
> Living and loving, all part of the game.
> If I had it to do over, I'd do the same.

It Takes Only One Other

You walk along the street,
    People glance your way
        Looking past you somewhere beyond
            Yet, seeing you not.

You are not alone on this street.
    People walk toward you
        Others with you, in the flow
            Yet, you are alone.

You may be on this street
    People nowhere in sight
        Alone with just one other
            Yet, fulfilled, complete.

November 1998

Limericks

There once was a boy named Billy
Who acted so gol-darned silly
He behaved like a clown
Did things upside down
And wrote what he felt Willy Nilly.

2/11/03

I once had a son named Chollie
He was so cute and jolly
He made everyone laugh
But he gave lots of gaff
He died very young by golly

2/11/03

I bought a bag of apricots
Thought I'd stew some, since there were lots
Fell asleep in my favorite chair
Smelled something burning, ran in to stare
Nothing was left but a blackened pot.

2/14/03

There was a girl named Shirley
Her hair was once red and curly
But it darkened with time
And since this line has to rhyme
This poem, as you'll note, ends early.

2/14/03

There once was a lady named Cindy
Who changed her name to Mindy
When questioned on this
She said, "You're amiss,
That was last week, now I'm Lindy."

2/18/03

Top O'the Mornin To Ye

It's March 17th, St Patty's Day is come round agin,
And I'll be wishin ye all, a merry old time.

May that little old leprechaun lead ye
To the pot of gold at the end of the rainbow.
May ye enjoy yer Red Mike and Lilacs
(Corned Beef and Cabbage) wit yer pint o'ale.

May ye git to kiss the Blarney Stone
And may ye git bunches of Shamrocks
This bonnie St. Patty's Day,
At the Wearin O'the Green.

Erin Go Bragh!

March 17, 2003

Summit Park

There is a park, Summit Park.
There is a hill on the opposite side.
At the top of the hill, I see large homes.
They call it The Summit.
Families live there.
There are flickering lights.
What goes on in those homes?
Are these happy homes?
Are there secrets, best unknown?
     I can only imagine.

Below in the park, there is grass.
There are trees of various kinds,
Some still green, some turning color.
It is autumn.
Mornings, people walk the paths.
Evenings, others bring their dogs, to meet, to run.
Saturdays, young people come to play ball.
Sundays, families come to picnic.
     This park is alive.

November 22, 2003

Grace Personified?

I had an acquaintance named Grace, who I thought was my friend. As couples we went out to dinner, followed by Operas, Concerts, and Theatres. We shared picnics at the beach and picnic suppers before outdoor summer theatres. I treated her nicely, included her in my family's functions. I paid her compliments which she graciously accepted, but never returned. When her husband, a true gentleman, died, my husband called her, as did I, to see how she fared. He asked if he could do something for her and there always was. I informed her when my husband died, but, she never called me once, to see how I was getting along. That hurt! I realized she was a social climber and never a true friend to me. When I moved away, I did not call to tell her I was going, nor have I called her since. She is out of my life. Sometimes she comes to mind and I wonder if she ever wonders what happened to me. Perhaps not! I wrote her off, as a selfish, self-centered (and I apologize for use of the word)   BITCH!

April 20, 2003

It Hurts

Do This! Try it! That's what "they" say.
No matter what, no matter how
I try, when comes the end of day,
The pains increase. Weight on foot, OW!
That hurts!! It's not their foot aches this way.
I want an instant cure, like now!

January 19, 1999

Lament

There is a vacancy in my heart,
where someone went away and left a hole.
A longing in my soul for that person
in his prime. Not, the someone just before
he sailed to unknown places;
bent, broken in body and spirit,
but the tall, upright man of our youth,
handsome, virile. Oh the Pity!
Gone, forever gone ……. Forsaken.

September 2, 1998

Love Remains

It's sad to lose your mate.
This, no one can deny.
So many years together,
Over, with a sigh.

One gets used to loss.
We have no other choice.
We can not change what is.
In this, we have no voice.

Still, our hearts hold on to love
And time can not dismiss
The feelings that we shared
When we sealed them with a kiss.

August 27, 2003

Where Are You Now?

Why aren't you here beside me?
Why aren't you standing where you once stood?
Why did you go away and leave me?
I'd bring you back, if only I could.
       Where are you now?

How can I find you, if I should look?
I don't want to be by myself.
How shall I start, which way should I go?
I didn't plan to be sitting alone on a shelf.
       Where are you now?

Oh, how I long for those earlier days,
When we were young, vibrant, carefree.
Oh, how I yearn for the good times we had.
I need not explain. I know you can see.
       But where are you now?

Tell me!
    Show me!
      Take my hand
        And lead me there
          To where you are.

December 31, 2003

My Wish

Making a wish is no guarantee that what I wish for will materialize. The way things are going, I don't feel at all optimistic. I have little confidence in the powers that be. I listen to them giving their reasons, their arguments for going to war. Although I agree with some of their reasoning, in my heart and in my gut, I am not for this war. My wish is for a miracle, that somehow the road we are on will have an off ramp and we will take that turnoff and avoid disaster.

March 8, 2003

2004

It's New Year's Eve. I'm here at home,
Drinking tea instead of Champaign,
Watching T.V., writing a poem.
I wouldn't call this fun, yet I can't complain.

I'm not dancing in an elegant gown,
Dining on foie gras or pheasant under glass.
Instead I'm in robe and slippers, sitting in my chair.
I can safely say it's a pain in the Ass.

Still, I've completed another year,
And here it is two thousand and four.
I'm alive. I'm productive, independent, free.
So, how can I ask for anything more.

December 31, 2003

I Love Flowers

When I was younger and more limber, I loved planting flowers in my garden. I enjoyed digging my hands in the soil. I enjoyed tending to my flowers and watching them grow. When they were in bloom, I loved cutting them, bringing them inside, and making beautiful flower arrangements. I allowed some of the flowers to dry and made arrangements of the dried flowers. I entered some of these, from time to time, at the County Fair and even won a First Prize with its Blue Ribbon.

Aside from the satisfaction of growing my garden, admiring and appreciating Nature's gifts, arranging the flowers in their fresh and dried state, my favorite of all is pressing the flowers at their peak. When they are dry and ready, I work them into pressed flower pictures. These one of a kind works of art, when framed and kept out of direct sunlight, will retain their color and last forever. The delicacy of the design and the colors, just go on blooming in my home. Whomever I give one of my pictures to as a gift, can enjoy the gift, long after the occasion for giving it has passed.

I also love painting flowers, and I love receiving them. Nowadays, I have only a raised flower bed around my patio. I try to keep it filled with seasonal flowers.

August 28, 2003

Not Today

What can one say about spring,
That poets have not said before?
Frankly, I can't think of a thing.
Shall I not write anything more?

No! There's got to be something new.
But what? "Come on Shirley, think!"
I'm thinking, my minds all askew.
Give up! It's a waste of ink.

There's always tomorrow. Right!?
Maybe, I'll wake with a spark.
Come up with a gem that's bright
And out of the impasse and dark.

Well, here it is next day at nine
And nothing developed, not a thing.
So, I will forget it for this time
And try it again, next spring.

April 8, 1997

An Acrostic

SHIRLEY

S he paints, she writes

H er talents are ongoing

I n many directions

R ight and left, one leads to another

L et her seek out new ways to be creative

E ach day brings forth new challenges

Y esterdays, she wrote, painted, designed,
   Today, this playful piece
   Tomorrow, who knows?

March 21, 2004

Springtime (An Acrostic)

S pringtime: everything comes to life,

P lants reawaken.

R oses begin to show their leaves; soon they will bud, then bloom.

I love it when winter comes to an end and the days are longer.

N ew greenery, new shoots.

G reen grass, green leaves, no more bare branches.

T rees send out new growth.

I feel rejuvenated when March 21st arrives, the first day of Spring.

M y heart sings when Spring is here.

E yes feast on the beautiful Spring flowers, as Spring springs forth.

March 21, 2004

White Roses

Yes, nature sleeps, under a blanket of snow
    when you live in a climate
      where snow falls.

Here in San Diego, I look outside
    no Christmas cactus do I see,
      only my white roses, in full bloom.

Most of my life, I lived
    in a place where cold came
      in winter, and snow grew and grew,

Just like my roses do here.
    Methinks I'd rather have
      roses than snow.

December 15, 1998

To My Dad

You've been gone so many years and I have shed abundant tears, missing you and realizing all we could have shared had you stayed on and continued to guide me.

I was only eighteen when you left that December twenty-sixth. I brought home two gowns for your approval, to wear on New Years Eve. You said, "They look so beautiful on you, keep them both. I never got the chance to wear either of them that New Years Eve, because you passed away so suddenly.

It was during Christmas vacation of my first year at the Traphagen School of Fashion. Being artistic yourself, you were so proud of my talent. I know that whatever talent I have, I owe directly to you.

So, on this Father's Day, I want to thank you for what you passed on to me and I want you to know that I wish you were still here, and I love you Daddy.

Your daughter,
Shirley
June 15, 2003

Let This Be My Prayer

Let this be my prayer.
Hear me from up above.
"Let me rise to where you are,
So we can meet again my love."

Hear my prayer, that's all I ask.
Then, maybe, it will come to be
"That, We will be together once more,
Until the end of time, just you and me."

April 11, 2004

Thoughts and Observations,
Or How to Make Time Pass

All along beside the train tracks, I see tall grasses that look like white feathered plumes. Chaparral, hills, and valleys, I wonder how many Native American moccasins walked this area. Some of these hills had to have been cut through when the railroad was built. Over the years, there has been erosion. Where possible, I see rocks and stones that have fallen. I don't see the ocean yet, though I know it is just beyond. I see the lagoon and then the sea comes into view. I am enclosed in a railroad car, yet I take a deep breath. Looking at the sea green water with its white foam, I feel I can smell the salt air. Ah! I am refreshed. Though on the chilly side, there are surfers out there, hardy souls these! "N.S.A.A." on a beach hut; what might it mean? National Surfers Association of America? As good a guess as any. People watching the surfers, here and there a seagull soars, sandpipers on the wet sand, all facing in the same direction to catch the sun, picnic tables and benches empty, on the beach people playing ball over a net.

We are nearing San Juan Capistrano. Quaint, pretty little storybook houses and gardens surround the railroad station. I look up at the sky, the prettiest shade of blue in between masses of white clouds. The edges of the clouds feather out until the white blends with the blue. How can I describe the blue? It is so clean and fresh. How can it be called "sky blue" when there are so many shades up there? I visualize the window as a frame.

What appears within the frame is a canvas. I study the sky. Up at the top the blue is darker. It fades to a pale gray blue where it meets the horizon. The sea, a dark teal blue, grows lighter and greener as it comes closer to shore, where it begins to break into gentle waves, which coax its sudsy foam onto the beach.

Santa Ana – what a pretty station! Red tiled roof, Mexican style. All around the building, midway on the walls, a border of colorful tiles. Below it , a checkerboard of blue and white and solid rust tiles. I see tall arched top windows, colonnades and a courtyard with fountain. I feel I am transported to a colonial Mexican village. Right after that scene, Hometown Buffet and McDonalds appear. I look for the beauty, but the ugly creeps in sometimes. Fields turned over, ready for early planting, approaching Santa Ana, more farms, rows with various shades of green. A man ambles along between the rows. He wears a white straw hat Mexican style; his hands in the pockets of his brown jacket. Next, I see fields of cabbages as we pull into the Irvine station.

Each scene is another painting. There is a condominium almost hidden by orange trees that grow around and between the buildings. What a clever idea! We bypass the city of Orange, round a bend and I can see the locomotive and the cars before mine, no two decorated alike. The conductor announces, "Fullerton in five minutes." Buildings with gang markings, a Budweiser building surrounded by many, many trucks and jeeps bearing its name, I can almost smell the beer. Fullerton station has lamp posts about every twenty feet with a big upright wreath and red bow surrounding its globe. In between each lamp post is a palm tree. A pretty sight! "Los Angeles in thirty minutes," comes over the loudspeaker. Do you want a three-hour train ride to go by fast? Start writing!

December 28, 1998

What Is My Destiny?

Have I already been there?
Have I achieved all that I'm capable of?
I'd hate to think that there is nothing more.

Surely, I can write one more poem.
Maybe that one poem will touch someone in ways I cannot fathom.
And because of it, I will be enriched.

If this is possible, then perhaps I have not yet fulfilled my destiny,
There is still more to be done, one more kind word to say.
One more smile to give to another, one more good deed to do.

One more picture to paint.
One more flower to grow.
And to see my book published.

As I write these encouraging thoughts, things to look forward to,
I feel uplifted,
And I know my destiny is still ahead of me.

My Thanksgiving Prayer

I am taking this time on Thanksgiving Day,
Though God knows I'm grateful everyday of the year.
Still I don't often stop what I'm doing to say,
"Thank you, dear God, for holding us near."

It's a good thing this day has been set apart,
To make us realize how lucky we are.
Our gratitude and appreciation come from the heart,
Just to live in this country, the greatest by far.

We ask you God, at this uncertain time,
To protect us from those who would do us harm.
Keep our country and our loved ones safe from crime.
Give us no cause for worry or alarm.

Let our people be lighthearted this Thanksgiving Day.
Let us be joyous yet thankful as we celebrate,
For our freedom, our families, all that we have and may,
We all say, "Thank you " to you for what you did create.

Happy Thanksgiving God.
        Happy Thanksgiving Everyone.
                And please God, let there be PEACE.

Courage

Let us have Courage,
    To live each day in this New Year,
        Bravely, wisely, with purpose.

Let us have Courage,
    To weather storms that may come our way,
        That we may learn from them.

Let us have Courage,
    To see with clarity, in depth of understanding,
        New issues as they arise.

Let us have Courage,
    To improve all facets of our being,
        Enabling us to become the best we can be.

Swashbuckler

Swashbuckler, that's what they called him. He was exactly what the name implied: handsome, dashing, devil-may-care, arrogant.

All eyes turned toward him, as he rode into town each time, on the back of Fella, his black stallion. Every maiden in the village adored this man, and he knew it. There wasn't one, who would not have ridden off with him, had he tossed his black hat on the ground before her. He had that animal magnetism that attracts.

This day, he blew into town, kicking up clouds of dust, laughing uproariously as he usually did. He pulled up the reins and came to an abrupt stop in front of the Golden Eagle Saloon. He jumped down, tied up his horse, stepped up to the doorway and with both hands threw open the wooden swinging doors and went inside.

"Cut! That wraps it up for today", called out the director.

January 28/29, 1999

The Restaurant Review

Have I got a place for you! It is the brand new restaurant, called "Elegance", and this one I have to give a well deserved Five Stars *****.

It is ideally located by the "Secluded Stream" with access from Sand Canyon Road. No longer does one have to travel downtown to enjoy a restaurant of this caliber.

Santa Clarita has long needed an up grade restaurant of this kind. There has not been anything close to it in this area, up until now.

There are tables outside under the trees, for those who prefer dining al Fresco. Tiny sparkling lights are laced through the trees and spotted throughout are unusual hanging cages with live singing birds.

Just approaching this place gives one the feeling of a wonderland with unexpected things to come. The building is surrounded by flower bordered walkways for strolling before or after dinner. How pleasant to sit on a bench, relax and listen to the birds joining in with the lovely music wafting out from inside the building.

Indoors, the décor is soft, pleasant and refined. The colors are pale pink, old rose and shades of mossy green. The tables are set with green cloths, pale pink china, old rose napkins and a centerpiece of green glass filled with pink roses. The carpet is a deeper shade of bronze green. The French chairs are covered in old rose velvet. Five violinists play a medley together, and then stroll to the tables to play requests.

Everything is immaculate, silverware polished to a high shine, glasses sparkle. The bathrooms faultless. Exactly what one would expect in an establishment of this kind.

The waiters attend to your every need and anticipate your wishes before you express them. Their uniforms are an extension of the décor: black trousers, pale pink shirt, black bow tie and a vertical striped vest of the pink and green shades and white gloves of course.

Continental food is served, and superbly, I might add. The food was pure perfection.

Last Saturday night, we were a party of four. We all ordered different appetizers and different entrees with wines to complement them. Everyone agreed that the food was unusually delicious and the presentation delightfully attractive.

As an example: My appetizer was Oysters Rockefeller. It was served in a silver hinged dish shaped like an oyster shell. The oysters sat on a bed of pink tinted rock salt. Nothing is overlooked.

My main dish was Duck a la Orange, laced with Grand Marnier. It was surrounded by baby vegetables, artistically arranged. Alongside it was a silver sauceboat with more of the sauce and fresh orange segments.

There was a cart, fashioned like a French flower cart, with eye appealing desserts, some of which were: fruit custard tarts, French pastries, cream puffs, a bowl of fresh fruit salad, chocolate whipped cream roll, and a platter of assorted cheeses with various-colored grapes. I had to forego these delights and settle for an aperitif. It was all just too good.

If you need to know the cost of such opulence, I suggest you call and speak to the Maitre D.

Fortunately, I was treated to this spectacular evening and I will go back, anytime someone is kind enough to invite me.

October 27, 2003

Halloween Is Over
And I For One Am Glad

It's a spooky season.
One has to have a reason
To dress up real wacky
And act like a fool, by cracky.

Normal people all year long,
On Halloween will act real silly,
Put on makeup and dress up ghoulish
And walk around looking stupid and foolish.

I wonder what prompts behavior like that.
When grownups let their hair down, dress like a cat,
What vicarious thrill do they get?
Oh, it's okay for kids, but, adults yet?

That's how it started, fun for the young folk,
But, when adults act like children that's no joke.
Children are supposed to learn from their betters.
Shouldn't parents be standard setters?

Maybe, they just never grew up.
Went on acting like an overgrown pup,
Need an excuse to revert to their youth,
Often behaving extremely uncouth.

Leave the cavorting to the girls and boys.
Let this be their time for candy and toys.
Hey Parents, don't cut in on the little one's page.
Help them enjoy it, but, you act your age.

November 1, 2003

Changing Clocks

Here we go again, Daylight Saving Time.
Okay, longer days, I like that.
But, then comes Fall.
Back to Standard Time.
Shorter days, I don't like that.

Changing clocks, timers, is a BOTHER.
Leave it alone, one way or the OTHER.

March 21, 2004

The Grocery Store

My parents owned a grocery store in Brooklyn, New York. Growing up, we each had duties to perform. When the Nabisco order came in, it was my job to set out the boxes of cookies and crackers on top of the refrigerated case. Another job I had was to go on Saturdays to a few customers, to take their orders. Then, I would come back to the store and fill those orders. My younger brother Morton would deliver the orders in a pushcart which we had for that purpose.

When groceries had to be unpacked on the shelves, Arthur, my older brother got up on the ladder and I handed the cans or boxes up to him. My dad reminded us to make sure the labels faced front.

Before coffee came in cans, already ground, we had two sacks of coffee. The tops were opened and rolled down and a scoop was placed in each bag. One was Medellin Bogotá, the other Santos. The customer put as much as he/she wanted in a paper bag. Whoever waited on the customer then weighed and ground the coffee in the coffee grinder. You could buy as much or as little as you wanted.

With the arrival of one pound cans of already ground coffee, this too was packed on the shelves. Though it was easier than weighing and grinding it was also a hazard. You had to grasp the can with a grab all stick and many a time one of us got hit on the head with a can of coffee, if we didn't grab it just right and hold on tight.

Before the era of the supermarkets, grocery stores were family owned and later on referred to as Mama and Papa stores. Many of these stores had rooms behind, where the family lived, not us. We had one large room that served as both store room and kitchen. There was no central heating. We had a pot-belly stove for heating. Daddy made a fire in the morning and added coal as the day progressed. We had a boiler for hot water which was heated by gas, and a gas range for cooking.

We had an apartment on the next block, on the second floor over Jahre's Candy Store. The main streets in the area were lined with family owned stores. Those families lived in the floor above the store and rented out the second floor. On the corner was a bakery, then a hardware store, barber shop, dry cleaner/tailor, Jahre's Candy/Ice Cream/Stationary/Newspaper Store, and on the corner a Bar and Grill. Across from the bakery was the butcher shop and diagonally across from the bakery was our grocery store at 407 De Kalb Avenue. The cross streets were residential, red brick four family walk-up houses.

Although we had an apartment and we slept there, bathed and dressed there, had only holiday dinners there with our relatives, I can truthfully say we did not live there. Our lives for the most part, other than school hours, were spent in the store and the room behind it. We were a close knit family, Daddy, Mama and four children. Our parents were always there for us, to help with school work, answer our questions, and sing with us. We were a happy family. We felt safe and we knew we were loved. We went to regular school, religious school and studied a musical instrument. We had a business, an apartment, a car, and plenty of food. These were Depression Years, so by some standards you might say we were well off. We sat down at the table to eat dinner as a family, in the kitchen behind the store, but when a customer came in, one of us had to get up and wait on him or her.

In this environment we grew and thrived. Arthur was attending St. John's School of Pharmacy, I was in my first year at the Traphagen School of Fashion, Morton was attending Boy's High School, and Phyllis was just six years old and in first grade. It was Christmas vacation, when Daddy died very suddenly. He was only forty-four years of age.

After the grieving and adjustment, Mama who was only forty-two, continued to run the business, with our help, though most of the burden fell on her, since we were all in school. There were times I wished we didn't have a store and could have a home life like my school friends did. When I expressed this wish to my mom, she would say, "It's the spirit that makes the home and not the things you see."

It was very hard on my mother. She sacrificed a lot, but she had a goal and that was to educate her children. She saw Arthur and Morton through Pharmacy School, me through Traphagen School, and Phyllis through New York University. Each of us became a professional, and all due to the perseverance and guidance of our parents. Education held high priority with them.

Our growing up years in the grocery store did not hinder us. In fact, it gave us a sense of values, a need for sharing and contributing, and I am convinced it helped us to be the people we became.

January 12, 2004

Para Siempre

Tú, cerca de mi
Yo, cerca de ti
Es todo lo que quiero,
Todo lo que necesitaré…Para Siempre.

Tú, cerca de mi
Yo, cerca de ti
Eso, es como estaba
Eso, es como quería que estar…Para Siempre.

Tú cerca de mi
Yo, cerca de ti
No más, como creía que estuvieramos
Ahora, solo en mi memoria…Para Siempre.

Spanish Version

For Always

You, near me
I, near you
It's all that I want
All that I will need…For Always.

You, near me
I, near you
That is how it was
That is the way I wanted it to be…For Always.

You, near me
I, near you
No more, the way I believed that we would be
Now, only in my memory…For Always.

English Version

December 11, 2002

El Tango Del Amor

Bailamos juntos como en un sueño.
Nadie existe
Solamente nosotros, los únicos.
Bailando en el pico del mundo.

En nuestro sueño
Bailamos sobre las olas
Lejos en el mar
Y no miramos atrás

Cuando viene la noche, volvemos
Bailando con las olas hacia la playa
Nuestro baile, el tango del amor.
Estos dias, en mis suenos, bailo con el todavia.

Spanish Version

The Tango Of Love

We dance together as in a dream.
No one exists,
Only us, the only ones
Dancing on top of the world.

In our dream
We dance over the waves
Far out to sea
And do not look back.

When night comes, we return
Dancing with the waves, toward shore,
Our dance, the tango of love.
These days in my dreams, I dance with him still.

English Version

December 31, 2002

Why?

Why did you go away and leave me?
Why did you leave me to battle life alone?
No one to help with things around the house that need doing
And if I can't correct them, they go undone. Frustration! Sadness!

I am not the first one to be left a widow
And I'm not in as bad a position as some.
My children no longer need my attention and care.
I am able to keep my head above water and stay afloat.

I should be and I am thankful that I am independent.
I feel sad for those who cannot fend for themselves
And they must go to others for sustenance.
They are the ones who need pity, not I.

There are always people everywhere, in any situation,
Who are "worse off"; But, on the other hand,
Some couples remain together for longer.
They have each other and that companionship

I am missing and deplore.
Yet again, there will come the time
When one of them will leave before the other
And the same loneliness, sadness, loss

That I feel, today, will befall the one who remains alone.
We have no choice but to accept what fate has dealt us.
But, still, we have feelings which surface from time to time.
And so we give vent to them.

November 1, 2003

I Remember

I remember the love.
Oh, how I recall that feeling.
Yes, he was sent from above,
To weaken my heart and set me reeling.

I remember the joys.
Oh, how I recall that pleasure.
Yes, we were like kid's toys,
Spinning and silly, yet we found lasting treasure.

I remember them still.
Oh, how I recall those years.
Yes, I'll remember until
There is no more breath in me or tears.

I remember, I remember, I'll never forget
Nor do I want to, nor will I try,
For too many memories won't let me forget.
I want to remember, till the day that I die.

January 12, 2003

I Wonder

I wonder if there will ever be another president of the caliber of Abraham Lincoln. It is amazing that a man, who started out with his humble beginnings, rose to become president of The United States, but he did become president, and a great one at that.

George Washington, our first president became known as "The Father of Our Country". On February 17th, we will celebrate Presidents Day, remembering the birthdays of these two great men. They were exceptional indeed, to be remembered and honored to this day.

Franklin Delano Roosevelt will go down in history as one of the greats, yet we do not celebrate his birthday. FDR was elected four times, and I voted for him each time, and had he continued to run, I would have gone on voting for him. That is the kind of faith I had in him as a president. Later on I learned things about him and I felt betrayed.

Not one of these modern day presidents since has inspired me in the same way. John F. Kennedy brought youth and hope to the presidency, but he was assassinated and served only one thousand days. He too did not bring to the people what was expected of him. Perhaps it is naïve to expect exemplary behavior from our president, a man after all, subject to human frailties.

What troubles me is that on Election Day, I do not feel that I am casting my vote for someone I really want to be our president. It seems I vote for the one who I think is the lesser of two evils, and it shouldn't be that way. And yet if there is a person out there who would make a wonderful president, and I'm sure there is, I can't blame him or her for not wanting any part of it.

We desperately need and want a strong leader, a person of high moral character, one who can inspire us all, to believe in that person's ability to lead the greatest country in the world.

I wonder: Will such a person come along in my lifetime?

February 17, 2003

Shiny Black Guitar

When he sat on the stool and sang
While strumming his shiny black guitar,
The sounds that came forth touched my heart
It was country music at its finest, by far.

I sang along with the words that I knew
As he picked those notes and strummed.
It didn't matter that the words were few
Those I didn't know, I just hummed.

The mellow sounds of that shiny black guitar,
How he fingered those strings sent tingles up my spine,
When he sang with that country twang
"My darling, come be my valentine."

No sight could have been more thrillin'
Than seeing him in his black Stetson, up there on that stage.
No sound could have been sweeter.
No wonder he is such a rage.

Clint Black is his name, and I wouldn't be surprised
If the shiny black guitar was deliberately selected
To match his surname. If so, that choice was wise,
For it captured my attention, which prompted
The writing of this poem.

February 25, 2003

It's My Country

I've traveled some and seen a lot
And everywhere there is much to see;
Places of historical interest and beautiful spots,
But the U.S.A. is the place for me.

Aside from the fact that I'm American born,
All I want and need is to be found right here.
If I had to live elsewhere, I would be torn
For the freedom I enjoy, to me is so dear.

People all over the world have national pride
Yet when I see hunger, poverty, and fear
I wonder, what have those folks to be happy about,
And I am ever so thankful that I live here!

March 20, 2003

Sisters

I had a sister, younger than me by twelve years.
For a long time, I was more like a mother to her.
She looked up to me, someone to emulate, learn from.

With time, she caught up. We married, had children,
A son and daughter each, and no longer did the age
difference matter.
Now we had so much in common and so much to share.

I gave her a book called "Sisters", pure sentiment.
She gave me a similar one, writing her personal thoughts
On how she felt about having me for a sister.

Not too long ago, she passed away.
What a void! What a loss!
I can't believe I no longer have a sister.

March 20, 2003

Come Swing In My Garden

Come, let's share our memories.
We'll swing high as we can go,
Maybe, even higher than the trees
And no one will ever know,

But us. When we tire of swinging
Then we can just sit and talk
And out of pure joy start singing
Or perhaps hold hands and walk

In my garden, among crocus and daffodils,
Iris and hyacinths, knowing spring is here.
We'll be happy as larks, look to the hills,
You and I together, with nothing to fear.

Yes, let's swing in my garden. You and I old friend
Think back to our youth, all we've been through.
Laughter and tears, remembrances without end,
But just stop and think, we're still here, me and you.

March 27, 2003

Deep In Your Eyes

When I look deep into your eyes
I see your soul
I see your heart
I see kindness and goodness
Humor, warmth and generosity.
I see you and I recognize the you of my dreams.
What do you see when you gaze into my eyes?
I hope you see in me
All that I behold in you.
It doesn't matter what others may see
When they look at each of us.
What does matter is
What we find and treasure in each other.
May we continue forever
To look deep into each other's eyes
And see our hearts and souls entwined.

April 9, 2003

Yesterday or Tomorrow

"Choose between yesterday and tomorrow.
Pick one and stick with it!" A quote from Elie Wiesel

Yesterday is gone, Kaput!
We can't bring it back, even if we should want to.
Maybe it is best forgotten, maybe not,
But it is over, finished.
All that is left of yesterday are the memories,
Some good, some not so good,
A part of our lives that is past.

Now, here we are today. We are alive!
Make the most of these hours. Embrace them!
Every moment is precious,
But, always keep in mind, there is a tomorrow.
Think of the possibilities that tomorrow may bring.
There is hope, a future to look forward to.
Choose tomorrow and be happy.

June 8, 2003

Independence Day
Port Washington New York

John Philip Sousa, The March King
  Who lived and wrote in our town
    Fills us with special pride
      When the bands march on down <u>MAIN STREET</u>

It's the Fourth of July
  And the whole town turns out
    Those who don't march
      Watch those who do, and line up along <u>MAIN STREET</u>

Wave flags, cheer, call out to their kids
  I do to my girl scout
    And my son the Fire Department volunteer
      As they march with their groups down <u>MAIN STREET</u>

The high school band, the police department
  The junior high band, the fire department
    The Polish Club in their colorful native costumes
      Keep on coming down <u>MAIN STREET</u>

It's a patriotic day, a festive day
  Neighbor greets neighbor, smiles abound
    Good times and fun, all around
      Till next year's parade on <u>MAIN STREET</u>

June 2003

Arthur

In 1959 at the age of forty-four my brother Arthur had a heart attack. We feared that he might suffer the same fate as his father, Harry, who at forty-four succumbed to coronary thrombosis, a fatal heart attack. During Arthur's illness and ultimate recovery, events in his life flashed through his mind.

Arthur was born on October 28, 1915, to Dora and Harry Greenberg, exactly nine months and four days after their marriage on January 24, 1915. He was a healthy serious-minded boy, giving his parents much pleasure. He was a good student and went through Elementary and High School easily and without incident. In school, he swam and played soccer and tennis.

Arthur had just turned twenty-one when in December of 1936, his father died suddenly. He had been planning to go to medical school in Ireland, but upon his father's death, he changed his mind and decided to go to St. John's School of Pharmacy, near his home. He didn't want to leave his mother alone, with a business to run and three younger children to raise. He felt he had to be close to his family to help out if he was needed.

After four years of study, he graduated Cum Laude with the degree of Bachelor of Science in Pharmacy. He went to work as a Pharmacist in the Boulevard Drug Store in Rockaway Beach, Arverne, N.Y. a resort town. Soon after he bought this store and ran it until he went into the Navy at the beginning of World

War II. In order to keep the business going so that he would have it to come back to after the war, I took a leave of absence from my job, hired pharmacists and ran the business during the summer, the peak season three years in a row.

When Arthur enlisted in the Navy, he was assigned as Pharmacist Mate on board the U.S.S. Raccoon, a tanker, and sent to the Pacific. Since he was the only medic on board his duties were many and he performed them well. The captain of the ship became very ill. Arthur treated him as best he could. He researched the illness and diagnosed it as Denghi Fever. He wired the command and a helicopter was sent to transport him to a hospital. He saved his captain's life. Because of this he was commended and sent back stateside for officer training.

He attended Colgate University. While on leave he met and then courted Doris Bandklayder. He went on to complete his studies at Notre Dame and became an Ensign. After he was released from the Navy he and Doris were married on June 12, 1945, their son Harry was born nine months and five days later on March 17, 1946. Arthur once again opened his store, but ran it only during the summers, and worked as a pharmacist in New York City, the rest of the year. They rented a small apartment in Arverne and set up housekeeping.

In 1950, Arthur and my husband as partners bought Bayles Pharmacy in Port Washington, Long Island, and we rented a small house together. Gina, Arthur and Doris's daughter was born on March 13, 1950. Arthur and my husband became Masons, joined the Temple and became solid citizens involved in community affairs. As the business prospered, Arthur and Doris took a day off each week, went into Manhattan, to museums, art galleries, dinners in fine restaurants, concerts and the theatre.

About five years later, we sold Bayles Pharmacy. Arthur bought Montauk Drug Store in Patchogue, Long Island, bought a beautiful home on Roe Boulevard, joined the Temple there, and began to make friends and socialize with the doctors in the community. Arthur bought a sailboat and enjoyed sailing with his children on Long Island Sound.

When in 1959 Arthur suffered his heart attack, Doris took over running the store, along with John Poulos, their pharmacist, until Arthur recuperated and was able to resume his normal life. Thereafter, Doris was always in the store with him helping to share the work load and giving him more time away from the store to rest and relax. Oddly enough, during his recuperation he took an interest in baking, one more thing that he excelled in, turning out wonderful pies and pastries. This and playing his violin, sustained him. He and Doris still went into the city each week to shop and to pursue his interest in the arts. He enjoyed going to Sotheby's Auctions and began to collect several important paintings. He loved to travel abroad.

He was a gentleman in the true sense of the word - handsome, impeccably dressed, intelligent, sensitive, and worldly. His friends recognized that in him and clung to him. His customers respected and trusted him, and his family adored him.

He was on a trip, had just arrived in Majorca, Spain, when he received a call that his mother had passed away. He returned home immediately. He had plans to take his mother on a trip to London and Israel, but it was not meant to be. When it came time to take that trip my husband and I went with him and Doris. That trip was one of the highlights of my life. Harry, Arthur and Doris's son who was in the Peace Corps in Africa, joined us in Israel and toured with us all seventeen days. He had studied in Israel earlier, and was very knowledgeable. So much so, that very often our guides stepped aside and asked Harry to conduct the lectures.

After Harry returned to Nairobi, Kenya, he wrote to his father concerning a bright young boy who could not afford to attend school. Arthur sponsored that boy making it possible for him to do so.

Arthur commissioned a well known sculptor, Perez by name, to create a lectern for his temple in Patchogue. He worked

299

with this artist every step of the way, from its inception to its dedication, seeing to every detail.

On October 6, 1972, Arthur and Doris went to bed, dreaming of their trip abroad, the following day. Arthur passed away quietly, in his sleep. He was fifty six years of age.

August 6, 2004

Yellow

Candle glow is yellow
Sunshine is yellow
And a bug light by the front door is yellow

    Sunflowers, pansies, chrysanthemums
    Daffodils, carnations, roses, all yellow
    Buttercups and many wildflowers are yellow

There are yellow school busses
And yellow taxicabs
And a Beatles song called Yellow Submarine

    A cat's yellow eyes
    Fuzzy yellow baby chicks
    And yellow marshmallow chicks at Easter

A cup of tea – yellow
Lemon pie – yellow
Two eggs, sunny side up – yellow

    You know spring is on its way
    When yellow crocuses
    Poke up through the snow.

Autumn leaves from pale yellow to deep gold
Form a carpet when they fall
Beneath the trees

Corn on the cob
Dripping in butter
Yellow---Yum!

A field of golden wheat
Bathed in summer's sun
Swaying in the breeze

Lemons, grapefruit, bananas
Pineapple, golden raisins
Golden Delicious Apples – Yellow!

Yellow Bell Peppers, yams
Yukon Gold Potatoes, yellow squash
Abundant yellow harvests.

Apple juice and cider
Many welcomed yellows come in fall.

Lemon drops, lemon sherbet
Lemonade and cold beer on a hot day
And hot chicken soup on a cold, cold day

Topaz: from pale yellow to smoky topaz
All kinds of gold jewelry
And yellow diamonds

Yellow curls I wore as a tot.
And a favorite yellow dress
I never forgot.

My faithful friend, the yellow legal pad
On which I scribble down my thoughts
Rewrite and revise.

Yellow is happy, yellow is bright
A morning color, never night
Though an evening sunset can be
Yellow too, and especially lovely
When streaked with blue.

After winter's cold and gloom
Sunshine's yellow brings warmth
And brightness into a room
And is so very welcome.

December 12, 2003

Be My Friend

I need you to be my friend.
I need for this friendship to never end.
We need to be together, forever and more,
And that still won't be enough time to store

Up memories to spare.
True friendship needs time to grow,
Time to mature, time to care,
Time to develop, time to share.

True friendship is love of a special kind,
Warm and glowing with peace of mind,
Never doubting, complete trust,
Believing in one another, that's a must.

So, what is a friend?
A brother, a sister,
A closeness that's true,
The kind of a friendship, like Me and You.

June 20, 2003

Fun At The Zoo

There were two tall giraffes.
I visited them often at the L.A. Zoo.
Seeing them both made me laugh.
One was pink, the other one blue.

I walked to see the Polar Bears.
Someone had painted them Emerald Green.
Seems they always keep them penned in pairs.
They dove into the pool and came up clean.

The chimps were surely a sight to behold
All in pastel shades, performing with ease,
Some quite young, others quite old,
Swinging from branches, among the trees.

At the elephant enclosure, I laughed some more.
They walked in a line, trunk to tail,
Each a different color, in all, twenty-four.
It looked so funny, a rainbow trail.

If you feel depressed or bored or blue
And think to yourself, "What will I do today?"
Get yourself dressed and head for the zoo.
You may see the animals put on a display.

Perhaps not in the colors I've described in this poem,
But they'll put on a show, you can be sure.
You'll want to return. Get out of your home
To have fun, again and again on the animal tour.

November 4, 2003

Shöne Blaue Augen

Heute ist blau mein herz
Wen ich gedenke an deine blaue augen,
Und wie ich diesen augen so viel geliebt habe.

Traurig bin ich heute
Und ich wein blaue trären
Denken an dir und deine blaue augen.

Wie ich wünsch das du wollst nachmals kommen
Und mir zurück bringen dein lieblich warm herz
Und deine shöne blaue augen.

German Version

Beautiful Blue Eyes

Today my heart is blue,
When I remember your blue eyes
And how I loved those eyes so very much.

Sad am I today
And I cry blue tears
Thinking of you and your blue eyes.

How I wish that you will come again
And bring back to me your lovely warm heart
And your beautiful blue eyes.

English Version

June 20, 2003

If

If I were an Eagle
I would fly to where you are.
If I were to fly and reach you
Even though it's very far,

Would you hold onto my wings
And come back with me to where I live?
And would you accept from me
      All the love I have to give?

If I were a Hawk
I would lie in wait for you.
I would fly to where I know you'd be
And teach you what you need to do.

I'd dig my talons
In your strong shoulders
And away we would glide together circling,
Then soaring to some far-off boulders.

September 10, 2003

Thanksgiving

Shiny red apples, nuts of all kinds,
Great big fat turkey and stuffing galore,
Assorted, fine pies, to blow our minds.
Wait up, wait up! Here comes more!

Mashed potatoes, candied yams and I'm told,
Cauliflower with a creamy white sauce,
Cranberries, Medjool dates, a Jell-O mold,
And Jeff's favorite green bean dish, of course.

As if that's not enough, there's cider and wines.
And salads and relishes of different kinds.
But before we indulge in this fabulous feast
We hold hands and give THANKS.   That's the very least

We can do to show our appreciation
For bringing us together to celebrate
The first Thanksgiving at the start of our nation.
And that's exactly what we did, before we ate.

September 20, 2003

Dora

Today it seems inconceivable that parents would send their thirteen year old daughter alone, to a strange land across the ocean. In 1908, it was not uncommon. America was the "Goldene Medina". Its streets were paved with gold. It was "The Promised Land". What would prompt loving parents to send their precious child, you may ask? Conditions in Kabesti, Austria at that time were not good. It was a small rural "shtel", (village), and not many opportunities there. They wanted a better life for their daughter. It must have been a hardship for them to raise the money for a "shifscarte" (passage), and to make the necessary arrangements for travel to the port of departure. In addition she had to be cared for upon arrival at her destination. Then there were the tearful "goodbyes". How could this young girl know then that except for her brother Samuel, who joined her in America later, she would never see any of her family again? Dora Altman arrived in New York City aboard the Mauritania. She came through Castle Garden Port of Entry, forerunner of Ellis Island. What must she have felt all alone, the first time away from the bosom of her family and the life she had known? She was met by a Mrs. Hacker, a person from her hometown. She stayed with this family until they found for her a "shtelling" (a suitable placement) with a family who lived in Brooklyn, New York.

The Maltinsky family consisted of mother, father, one daughter and three sons. They owned the Central Ice Cream

Company on Maujer Street. On the corner was the ice cream parlor. The family lived on the floor above…behind it was the wholesale ice cream plant. Dora worked in the store and helped Mrs. Maltinsky in the house. She must have received a small salary in addition to room and board because she did send some money home and even made occasional deposits into a savings account at Adolph Mandel Bank. She knew the value of a dollar and was careful how she managed what little she had.

The Maltinsky family loved Dora. She was like a daughter to them. In fact they hoped that one day she would marry one of their sons.

Dora worked hard being anxious to succeed. She went to school at night to learn to improve her English. The Maltinsky children helped her. Eventually, she lost all traces of an accent. She came to love her surrogate parents, but as far as she was concerned, the boys were brothers.

Dora's parents always felt that she would save money, return home, marry there, and settle down. In their letters to her, they told how they missed her and longed for the day when she would return. It wasn't meant to be. I thank God that she did not, because she would have ended up dead like the rest of her family, thanks to Hitler and the Holocaust. Besides, I would not be telling her story.

Dora was my mother. Five feet high and petite, but, she stood straight, tall and proud. You can see it in her bearing, in pictures taken periodically to send to her family. She was a serious minded young woman and determined to be independent.

With a minimal amount of spare time and with limited resources, she did not indulge in frivolities. She associated with several cousins who came to the United States around the same time that she did, and for the same reasons.

She lived with the Maltinskys for seven years, until at twenty she married my father. A fine gentleman would come into the ice cream parlor and engage Dora in conversation. Over time she learned that he had a son and it became evident that he wanted them to meet. Harry was a sergeant in the quartermaster corps of the U.S. Army, stationed in Fort Adams Rhode Island. Mr. Greenberg brought his son into the ice cream shop when he came home on leave and introduced him to Dora. The rest is history.

I have the first letter he wrote to "My Dear Miss Altman", asking to see her, and all the letters and cards he sent her during their courtship from the formal opening of that first letter to the last which began with "My Own Dear Heart". She kept his letters but destroyed the ones she wrote to him, feeling that she was unable to write as beautifully as he did.

Mrs. Maltinsky later said, "As soon as he walked into the store I knew that, he was the Angel of Death and Dora would never marry one of my sons." Harry and Dora were married on January 24, 1915, soon after his discharge from the army. I prefer to think of Harry not as the Angle of Death, but the Angel of Life because Had Dora not fallen in love with and married him, she may have been encouraged by her parents to return home, and Dora would have met the same fate as her family.

Theirs was a true love affair for twenty two years, until at age forty-four, my father died suddenly. My mother was forty-two. She never remarried. I remember that there were men who tried to get her to go out with them but she never did. She felt that "No one could take Harry's place".

With Harry gone her children became her obsession... educating them, her #1 priority. She did not want to take the chance that a man might want her but not her children, might resent them, not treat them right, and she became the selfless mother I knew. Her children's achievements were her achievements, their talents their successes were her pride.

November 17, 1999

About the Author

Shirley Newman was born and grew up in Brooklyn, New York. After graduating from Erasmus Hall High School, she entered the Traphagen School of Fashion in New York City to begin a two year course in Costume Design and Fashion Illustration.

Upon completion of her studies, she concentrated on designing textiles. She worked for some of the finest textile firms in New York City. For many years she specialized in designing men's neckwear fabrics. After marriage and while raising her two children, she continued to do freelance designing.

Newman's second career was in the Port Washington, New York School System teaching Special Education to learning disabled students. In 1983, she moved to San Diego, California and continued taking courses at San Diego State University, graduating with honors. In 1997 she began attending a Creative Writing Class and continued until she moved to Valencia, California in 2001. Soon after, she joined a Writing Class there.

Newman has been published in the San Diego Writers/ Editors Guild Publication many times. Her poems and short stories have been published in several Senior's magazines as well as Santa Clarita's, "The Mighty Oak". She has also been published often in her temple's newsletter, "The Shofar". To date, she has written over two hundred fifty poems and memoirs and hopes to have her book published in the coming year.

Order Form

A String of Beads
By Shirley Newman
ISBN: 978-1-4269-1967-1
$19.95 (plus shipping per book)

Please ship my order to: (USA only)

Name _____

Street address _____

City _____

State _____

Zip _____

Phone _____

Submit check or money order for $19.95 (add sales tax if applicable) and $3.95 S+H per book to:

Temple Press
24015 Arroyo Park Drive #44
Valencia, CA 91355-3735